MONTAIGNE'S
ESSAIS

A STUDY

MONTAIGNE'S
ESSAIS

A STUDY

❦

DONALD M. FRAME

PRENTICE-HALL, INC.   ENGLEWOOD CLIFFS, N.J.

Printed in the United States of America

ISBN: C-0-13-600619-1
P-0-13-600627-2

Library of Congress Catalog Card No.: 69-15330

10   9   8   7   6   5   4   3   2

PRENTICE-HALL INTERNATIONAL, INC. (*London*)
PRENTICE-HALL OF AUSTRALIA, PTY. LTD. (*Sydney*)
PRENTICE-HALL OF CANADA, LTD. (*Toronto*)
PRENTICE-HALL OF INDIA PRIVATE LIMITED (*New Delhi*)
PRENTICE-HALL OF JAPAN, INC. (*Tokyo*)

⋈ ACKNOWLEDGMENTS ⋈

I am glad to acknowledge three debts. The English translations of Montaigne, which are my own, are reprinted from my translation, *The Complete Works of Montaigne* (copyright © 1948, 1957, 1958 by the Board of Trustees of Leland Stanford Junior University) with the permission of the publishers, Stanford University Press. In preparing this book I have drawn heavily on two earlier longer studies of Montaigne: for chapters III–VI, on *Montaigne's Discovery of Man: The Humanization of a Humanist* (New York: Columbia University Press, 1955); for chapters II–VII and XI, on *Montaigne: A Biography* (New York: Harcourt, Brace & World, Inc., 1965).

⋘ CONTENTS ⋙

I.	THE BOOK	1
II.	THE AUTHOR AND HIS TIME	4
III.	THE DECISION TO WRITE	16
IV.	SKEPTICISM: TEMPER AND TOOL	22
V.	THE SUBJECT AS SELF: THE ESSAY	32
VI.	THE SUBJECT AS MAN: BOOK III	42
VII.	THE FINAL ADDITIONS	53
VIII.	RELIGION	65
IX.	THE *ESSAIS:* CONCEPT AND STRUCTURE	72
X.	STYLE	86
XI.	DESTINY	97
APPENDIX I: CHRONOLOGY		105
APPENDIX II: FURTHER READING		107
NOTES		109
INDEX		116

❧ I ❧

THE BOOK

The first readers of Montaigne's *Essais* in 1580 faced two octavo volumes, published by Simon Millanges in Bordeaux, of 496 and 650 pages respectively. Two volumes, two books, divided not into essays but into chapters: 57 in Book I, 37 in Book II. Many of these were very short, no more than a page or two; some were long, such as those on education (Book I: ch. 26), presumption (II: 17), and the resemblance of children to fathers (II: 37); one giant, the "Apologie de Raimond Sebond" ["Apology for Raymond Sebond"] (II: 12), almost five times as long as any other, filled almost one fourth of the entire work. The title page read: ESSAIS DE MES-SIRE MICHEL SEIGNEUR DE MONTAIGNE, CHEVALIER DE L'ORDRE du Roy, & Gentil-homme ordinaire de sa Chambre.

In 1582 the same publisher brought out a second edition in one octavo volume with a modest scattering of additions to some chapters. Five years later the same version was republished by Jean Richer in Paris in one duodecimo volume. That there was an intervening third edition, now lost, probably in 1584, is suggested by one contemporary and by the fact that the second one after it is presented as the fifth.

This is the handsome quarto volume of about a thousand pages published by Abel L'Angelier in Paris in 1588, "augmented by a third book and by six hundred additions to the first two." Here for the first time are all three books and—with the 13 new chapters of Book III—all 107 chapters that we know; Montaigne added no more of either later.

However, in the remaining four years of his life (1588–92) he continued to work over this book that he called consubstantial with its author. On the unbound pages of a copy of the 1588 edition he

1

added about a thousand passages, from a word or two to several pages in length, in the spacious margins or, when he lacked room there, on separate slips of paper. These passages make up about one fourth of the entire work; this copy is now known as the Bordeaux Copy.

Three years after his death his "covenant daughter" (unofficial "adopted daughter" by mutual agreement) and literary executrix, Marie de Gournay, with the help of his friend Pierre de Brach, published a new edition, based—perhaps indirectly—on the Bordeaux Copy, in one folio volume in Paris, again with L'Angelier.

Since all these texts are of course extremely rare and costly, students of Montaigne may be grateful for three modern reproductions: the Dezeimeris and Barckhausen edition (Bordeaux: Gounouilhou, 1870–73, 2 vols.), which reproduces the 1580 text (Books I and II) with all the variants of 1582 and 1587 and shows where further changes were made later; the Edition Phototypique of the Bordeaux Copy (Paris: Hachette, 1912, 1024 plates); and the Edition Municipale (Bordeaux: Pech, 1906–33, 5 vols.) by Strowski and others, which gives all the variants of the basic texts of the *Essais*.

Nowadays the *Essais* usually appear in scholarly readers' editions, based primarily on the Bordeaux Copy and secondarily on the 1595 edition, like those of Villey, Plattard, Thibaudet, and M. Maurice Rat, whose Pléiade text of Montaigne's *Œuvres complètes* is the French edition of reference for the present book.[1] These add four elements not found in the basic texts: (1) paragraph breaks, not used by Montaigne and his publishers; (2) translations and sources of the myriad quotations in prose and verse (mainly Latin) with which Montaigne studded his book; (3) footnotes or backnotes; and (4) strata indicators. These last are usually forms of the letters A, B, and C, set off in various ways from the text, which show that the passages that follow them first appeared in 1580, 1582, or 1587 (A), in 1588 (B), or after 1588 (C). They are often indispensable for following the movement of Montaigne's thought.

All these appurtenances were absent from the early versions. A reader of the first edition—to return to him—would have learned that Montaigne was a lord, a wearer of the collar of St. Michael ("*l'ordre du Roy*"), and a gentleman of the chamber in ordinary to King Henry III, but would probably not have known that he was of fourth-generation nobility, son of a recent mayor of Bordeaux, member of the prosperous Eyquem family (their bourgeois name, which Michel was the first to drop), gentleman in ordinary also to Henry of Navarre (the future Henry IV), former councillor (for thirteen years) in the Parlement of Bordeaux, who had heretofore published only a translation (1569) of Raymond Sebond's *Natural Theology* and a series of dedicatory letters to the posthumous works of his friend Etienne de La Boétie.

If Montaigne's listing of his distinctions was designed to present his work as that of a gentleman amateur, the same is even truer of his title, which he invented and was the first to use. He describes but never defines it; his book must serve as the definition. Of its diverse meanings, more later; enough for now that it was very different from its main antecedents—the relatively impersonal *Moralia* (since Montaigne's time sometimes called *Moral Essays*) of his beloved Plutarch, the *Discourses* of Machiavelli, and the many anecdotal books of *diverses leçons* (varied readings) that flourished in sixteenth-century France—and that Montaigne seems to have had two main overlapping meanings in mind, related to his subject of self-study, of which the *Essais* were rather the method than the vehicle: tests or trials of his judgment, the instrument of self-study; and probings and samplings of that self.

Thus it was a novel subject and a novel book that greeted the reader eight years after the St. Bartholomew's Day Massacre. Surprisingly, it was well received from the first—not a best seller, but a solid success, as the repeated new editions show. Less surprisingly, and ironically, the main reasons for this success seem to have been not Montaigne's original insights but rather the formidable erudition which he was so eager to disclaim. At all events, the book was read; the self-portrait was received without ridicule; and a few distinguished readers like La Croix du Maine and Justus Lipsius hailed the author as another Plutarch and as "the French Thales."

~§ II §~

THE AUTHOR AND HIS TIME

The time was ugly. The splendor of the French Renaissance had been bloodied by the savagery of the religious civil wars, which had been raging for eighteen years when Montaigne's first *Essais* appeared. Four years later, when in 1584 the Protestant leader Henry of Navarre became heir to the throne of France, the extremist Catholics of the Holy League, led by Henri de Guise, became a third party opposed to the crown unless in control of it. In 1588, when the first three-book edition of the *Essais* was published, Henry III was a virtual prisoner of Guise in Paris in May, and in December had him killed. Within a year it was his own turn to die, at the hands of an assassin. Montaigne did not live to see Navarre, successor to Henry III as Henry IV, either crowned or admitted inside his capital of Paris.

The early years of the century had been glorious ones for France. Francis I, who loved pleasure, women, the arts, and the sport of warfare, had continued the luxury of expansionist wars in Italy, politically and militarily weak and divided but the leader of Europe in culture. Though his defeat at Pavia (1525) and ensuing one-year imprisonment by his great rival Charles V, Emperor of the Holy Roman Empire, was a blow to his warlike ardor, he continued his generous patronage of the arts, bringing from Italy countless treasures and such artists as Leonardo and Cellini. For over half of his thirty-two-year reign (1515–47) he supported the leading writers, who were mostly moderate religious reformists (like Marot and Rabelais), against the attacks of the conservative theologians of the Sorbonne; and he never abandoned his creation, the Collège des Lecteurs Royaux (future Collège de France), the first nontheological school of higher learning in France.

On the night of October 17–18, 1534, however, handbills violently attacking the Papacy and the Mass were posted all over Paris and even on the king's chamber door in Amboise. From the time of the Affaire des Placards, as this was called, Francis turned against the generally Erasmian moderate reformists and treated them as seditious heretics. One result of the reprisals that followed was Calvin's publication of his *Institutes* and flight to Geneva (1536), which he built into a citadel of militant Protestantism. Persecution remained severe in France and grew more intense under Henry II (1547–59); but French Protestantism, previously ineffective in its Lutheran form, under Calvin's influence became a solid underground force.

Since the accession of Charles V as Emperor in 1519, France's principal foreign policy had been the struggle with the Holy Roman Empire for European hegemony. Though much of the fighting took place in Italy, the ultimate aim was victory over the German and Spanish Imperials. Events of the latter 1550's, however, prepared a new phase of the rivalry. Charles V abdicated as King of Spain and Emperor in 1555–56 in favor of his son Philip II and brother Ferdinand I, and retired to spend his last days in a monastery; the treaty of Cateau-Cambrésis (1559) virtually ended French foreign wars for the rest of the century; and the death of Henry II (1559), followed in the next year by that of his eldest son Francis II, left the crown to the ten-year-old Charles IX and the major influence to his foreign-born mother, Henry II's widow, Catherine de' Medici.

The weakness of the monarchy led to a power struggle involving major princes and nobles. A conspiracy against the Guises in 1560 was foiled and harshly punished. An attempt to reconcile religious differences by the Colloquy of Poissy (1561) completely failed. Early in 1562 the religious civil wars broke out, to rage, with occasional interruptions, for thirty-two years.

Many of the combatants, especially the leaders, lacked deep conviction; and the Protestants, never more than a small minority in Catholic France, did not win an important battle for twenty-five years. But revenge and ambition were sufficient motives; and the depletion of the royal treasury often kept the king from achieving a decisive victory. Moreover, after the bloodbath of St. Bartholo-

mew's Day (August 23–24, 1572) had failed to end Protestant resistance, the crown found itself more and more often in the middle
of a struggle with extremists on either side. The ultra-Catholic Holy
League, led by the Guises, was formed in 1576; in 1584 the death of
the king's last brother made Henry of Navarre, the Protestant leader,
heir to the throne with the king's support; the League put forward
a rival heir; and the eighth civil war, the War of the Three Henries,
led the government and the Protestants, as loyalists, to join forces
against the League. After the two killings, of Guise by Henry III in
1588, of Henry III by a fanatic monk in 1589, Henry of Navarre,
now Henry IV of France, was left with a small army to try to win
his kingdom from the vastly superior forces of the League. Only
after he abjured his Protestantism for the second time (1593) was
he crowned and allowed to enter Paris (1594). Only four years later,
by the Edict of Nantes (1598), did the Protestants gain religious
freedom and political rights.

Montaigne spent the last thirty years of his life in the midst of
these wars. A stanch Catholic loyalist, he was also a fair-minded
moderate of good will and a friend and admirer of Henry of
Navarre. As mayor of Bordeaux he worked hard and well to keep
the city peaceful and loyal; during the siege of Castillon he was, as
he puts it (III: 12, 1021, S798–99), belabored from both sides, a
Guelph to the Ghibellines, a Ghibelline to the Guelphs; he was
nearly driven from his château once, held up and robbed twice,
imprisoned once. Such were the times. His own testimony is eloquent.

*Je me suis couché mille foys chez moy, imaginant qu'on me trahiroit
et assommeroit cette nuict là . . . (III: 9, 948, S741.)*

*Monstrueuse guerre . . . Elle vient guarir la sedition et en est
pleine, veut chastier la desobeyssance et en montre l'exemple . . .
aucune partye n'est exempte de corruption. (III: 12, 1018, S796.)*

*Confessons la verité: qui trieroit de l'armée, mesmes legitime et
moienne, ceux qui y marchent par le seul zele d'une affection religieuse, et encore ceux qui regardent seulement la protection des loix
de leur pays ou service du Prince, il n'en sçauroit bastir une com-
paignie de gensdarmes complete. . . . Nous ne prestons volontiers
à la devotion que les offices qui flattent noz passions. Il n'est point
d'hostilité excellente comme la chrestienne. Nostre zele faict merveilles,
quand il va secondant nostre pente vers la haine, la cruauté,
l'ambition, l'avarice, la detraction, la rebellion. A contrepoil, vers*

la bonté, la benignité, la temperance, si, comme par miracle, quelque
rare complexion ne l'y porte, il ne va ny de pied, ny d'aile. Nostre
religion est faicte pour extirper les vices; elle les couvre, les nourrit,
les incite. (II: 12, 420–21, S323–24.)

[I have gone to bed a thousand times in my own home, imagining
that someone would betray me and slaughter me that very night . . .

Monstrous war! . . . It comes to cure sedition and is full of it,
would chastise disobedience and sets the example of it. . . . No part
is free from corruption.

Let us confess the truth: if anyone should sift out of the army,
even the average loyalist army, those who march in it from the pure
zeal of affection for religion, and also those who consider only the
protection of the laws of their country or the service of their prince,
he could not make up one complete company of men-at-arms out of
them. . . . We willingly accord to piety only the services that flatter
our passions. There is no hostility that excels Christian hostility.
Our zeal does wonders when it is seconding our leaning toward
hatred, cruelty, ambition, avarice, detraction, rebellion. Against the
grain, toward goodness, benignity, moderation, unless as by a miracle
some rare nature bears it, it will neither walk nor fly. Our religion
is made to extirpate vices; it covers them, fosters them, incites
them.]

Montaigne's father's family, the Eyquems, can be traced to Bordeaux as far back as the tenth century. Hard-working, prosperous
dealers in the local commodities of salt fish, wine, and the dyestuff
woad, they were important citizens of Bordeaux by the fourteenth
century. In 1477 Montaigne's great-grandfather Ramon Eyquem
bought the noble house and land of Montaigne, just north of the
Dordogne River where Périgord meets Guienne, and thus became
the first nobleman in what was thenceforth the Eyquem de Montaigne family. In the next generation and especially the one after
that, the family moved steadily away from business into careers
more appropriate for nobles: arms, law and government, the church.
Montaigne's father, Pierre Eyquem (1495–1568), fought in the Italian wars and served as jurat, provost, deputy mayor, and mayor of
Bordeaux.

The family of Michel's mother, Antoinette de Louppes, were
distinguished and prosperous marranos, or converted Spanish Jews;
a great-great-great-grandfather of Montaigne, Micer Pablo Lopez
de Villanueva, was burned at the stake by the Inquisition. When
the Jews were banished from Spain by Ferdinand and Isabella in

1492, Montaigne's maternal grandfather, Pierre de Louppes, settled
—and soon prospered—in Toulouse. His brother Antoine, who
established himself in Bordeaux, had business dealings with the
Eyquems and was probably the one who arranged the marriage of
Montaigne's parents in 1529. Michel was the third child born but
the oldest who survived to maturity.

Though thrifty and hard-working, Montaigne's mother seems to
have lacked warmth. It was his father, able, generous, and kind,
that he adored.

The surviving children were eight in number: five sons, three
daughters. The most striking feature of the family is its deep unity
beneath the diversity of its religious convictions; for one brother
and one sister were Protestants.[1] In a period of fierce religious
passions that set brother against brother, son against father, Pierre
de Montaigne, a firm Catholic, practiced full religious tolerance
within his family. Obviously for him freedom of conscience was
essential.

Michel de Montaigne was born on February 28, 1533, in the
Château de Montaigne, set on a sort of plateau a few miles north
of the Dordogne and about thirty miles east of Bordeaux.[2] It was a
spacious yellow-gray red-roofed manor built around a large square
courtyard, with towers at two adjacent corners connected by walls
with each other and with the main building to the west, which was
fronted by a handsome terrace with a fine view over the valley of
the little Lidoire to the hills and castles to the west and north. His
birth was anxiously awaited, since two older children had died and
his mother had carried him for eleven months. His father, born on
Michaelmas Day (September 29) must have chosen his name, and
generally called him by his nickname Micheau.

To bring him close to the humble, Pierre Eyquem had him held
over the baptismal font by peasants and sent out to nurse with them
—a plan which his son commends as successful (III: 13, 1079, S844).
Back home, he was brought up gently, without rigor or constraint,
feeling the rod only twice, and that softly (II: 8, 368–69, S281), and
awakened each day by the sound of music. Put in the care of a tutor who spoke Latin but no French, and of two assistants, he heard
no French until he was six and learned Latin as a mother tongue.

He was then sent to the illustrious young Collège de Guyenne, one of the finest schools in France, where he played the lead in several Latin plays and showed such fluency in that language that even eminent Latinists on the faculty feared to accost him. He finished the twelve-year course in seven years, but with little to show for it beyond a hatred for rigor and violence in education. However, it may well have been here and in his later youthful studies that his mind formed the habit by which pagan culture and speculation coexist happily with Christian belief.[3]

His next years, from thirteen to twenty-one or twenty-four, are unknown to us. He may have had some free time in Paris, possibly studying with one or more of the Lecteurs Royaux; he may well have studied law at the University of Toulouse. In 1554 his uncle Pierre de Gaujac bought himself a councillor's position in a new tax court, the Cour des Aides of Périgueux. When it was suppressed two and a half years later, and its members, in compensation, incorporated into the Bordeaux Parlement, Gaujac had resigned his seat to his favorite nephew; but whether Michel actually served in Périgueux we do not know.

For the next thirteen years, from 1557 to 1570, Montaigne was a councillor in the Bordeaux Parlement. This was one of eight bodies composing *the* Parlement, the highest court of justice in France, which also had some say in policy, especially when the crown was weak, and in administration, where, as the arm of the king, it often supplanted the nobility and local officials. Montaigne served in two of its minor chambers, the Chambre des Requêtes and then the Chambre des Enquêtes; the higher chambers were barred to him by the presence of close relatives. Often a vehement spokesman for the newcomers from Périgueux, who were grudgingly received and long shabbily treated, he seems to have been a conscientious but unenthusiastic magistrate. As he came to see the inadequacy of human law, he formed a skeptical view of the achievements of the human mind.

One good thing came out of his years in the Parlement: the closest tie Montaigne ever formed, his friendship with Etienne de La Boétie, a colleague two years older, married to a woman older than himself. A dedicated public servant, highly regarded by his colleagues, La Boétie was erudite, at home in Greek as well as

Latin, the author—as yet unpublished—of distinguished works in prose and verse. They met soon after Montaigne came to the Parlement, having already "embraced each other" by their reputations, and promptly formed a friendship which both considered unique. Based in part on a deep love of antiquity, it sought to emulate classic friendships, was conceived as an elective brotherhood, and met both men's deep need for the fullest possible communication. In August, 1563, La Boétie fell ill of dysentery, and nine days later died a most courageous and Christian death. Montaigne, who was with him throughout his illness, never ceased to mourn him. La Boétie's bravery showed him how well a man could confront death, and drew him for about ten years toward the rather Stoical attitude of his friend. The loss of full communication helped lead him to write his *Essais*.

After seeking diversion from his grief in various amours, Montaigne let himself be married in 1565, at the age of thirty-two to her twenty, to Françoise de La Chassaigne, daughter and granddaughter of distinguished members of the Bordeaux Parlement. He regarded love and marriage as incompatible, and says he would have avoided marrying Wisdom herself if she had wanted him. His wife bore him six children, all girls, of whom only one, Léonor, survived infancy, growing up to marry twice and continue the family line. Theirs seems to have been usually an amiable household, but not always; though Montaigne depicts himself as alternately loving and cool toward his wife, he lists among his reasons for liking to travel *"le soulier neuf et bien formé de cet homme du temps passé, qui vous blesse le pied"* ["the new and well-shaped shoe of the man of days gone by, which hurts your foot"] (III: 9, 925, S723), an allusion to a story told twice by Plutarch. A Roman, admonished by friends for having divorced his beautiful, discreet, and fruitful wife, pointed to his handsome new shoe, which pinched, and explained that this represented the myriad trivial annoyances that made his wife impossible to live with. At best a dutiful husband, Montaigne behaved better in marriage, and found it better, than he had expected; but it offered him fewer roses than thorns.

About two years after his wedding his father set him a novel task. Over twenty years earlier, a guest had given Pierre de Montaigne a book considered a bulwark against Protestantism and atheism, the

Liber Creaturarum, sive Theologia Naturalis (Book of the Creatures, or Natural Theology) of the fifteenth-century Spaniard Raymond Sebond. Written in clumsy medieval Latin, it sought to prove the existence and nature of God by analogies drawn from the levels of his creation. Pierre de Montaigne's youthful Latin had grown rusty; he presumably wanted to draw his son into some useful and congenial line of endeavor; he asked him to translate it, liked what he saw of the result, and arranged to have it published. Montaigne proved an excellent translator of Sebond's thousand pages, holding faithfully to the sense even as he livened up the pedestrian style and gave it color and freshness. However, his version of the Prologue, which—alone—was on the Index of Prohibited Books, deliberately cuts down Sebond's extravagant claims for his book, which emerges no longer as *infallible* and *necessary*, but as a potentially useful guide on the way to religious truth. Though Montaigne may well have sought in this way to demonstrate his own orthodoxy, his deliberate mistranslation of the Prologue shows his skepticism already about Sebond's powers and claims.

As Montaigne, in Paris, addressed the preface of his translation to his father, Pierre de Montaigne, after seven years of torment from the kidney stone, lay dying at Montaigne. Michel returned home promptly and worked out the settlement of the estate—easily with his brothers, not so easily with his mother. He was now Lord of Montaigne, head of the family, owner of the château and the estate. A year later he sought promotion to a higher chamber in the Bordeaux Parlement, was refused because close relatives were there, and rather than seek a dispensation from the king, chose to resign, presently selling his position (in the manner of the time) to a younger friend. Much of the year 1570, when this transaction was completed, was spent in collecting La Boétie's works and having them published in Paris, severally, with dedications by Montaigne to eminent prospective guardians of his friend's memory. This done, back in Montaigne, he celebrated his thirty-eighth birthday (February 28, 1571) by having an inscription painted on the wall of a little room next to his library-study, commemorating his retirement to freedom and tranquillity in the bosom of the Muses. Within a year he had started writing his book.

In his large château one place was all his own: his study on the third floor of his famous tower.[4] It was a homey, rounded room, well lighted, with windows looking out in three directions. On the beams of the ceiling Montaigne had inscribed fifty-odd Greek and Latin quotations, most of them summing up the frailty and ignorance of man. Five rows of shelves on all sides held his handsome library of a thousand books.

Là, je feuillette à cette heure un livre, à cette heure un autre, sans ordre et sans dessein, à pieces descousues; tantost je resve, tantost j'enregistre et dicte, en me promenant, mes songes que voicy. (III: 3, 806, S629.)

[There I leaf through now one book, now another, without order and without plan, by disconnected fragments. One moment I muse, another moment I set down or dictate, walking back and forth, these fancies of mine that you see here.]

How the book took shape, and the shape it took, will be the concern of our next five chapters. Nine years after Montaigne's retirement, in 1580, Books I–II were published in Bordeaux in the two volumes already described. Over those nine years Montaigne had worked steadily, gaining speed and sureness as he went on.

Meanwhile his life was not all spent in his tower. His love of the outdoors shows in almost every word he writes. Horseback riding he loved, and he spent much of his life in the saddle, where, he tells us (III: 5, 854, S668), his thoughts ranged most widely and fruitfully. Travel he loved for its own sweet sake. In his years in the Parlement he had made the trip to Paris and the court often, apparently about once a year, and not always on Parlement business. Judging from his two titles, the Order of St. Michael (1571) and gentleman in ordinary of the king's chamber (1573 or earlier), he must have already enjoyed some esteem at court. Much more significant is the episode, reported by his friend Jacques-Auguste de Thou, a careful historian, as told him by Montaigne himself, in which Montaigne sought to mediate between Henry of Navarre and Henri de Guise while both were at court—that is, between 1572 and 1576. Though the attempt, probably sponsored by the queen mother, Catherine de' Medici, was foredoomed, it shows confidence already among the great in Montaigne's fairmindedness and good will toward both sides.

His book published and a copy of it presented to King Henry III, who received it graciously, Montaigne went north in June, 1580, served in the king's army at the siege of Protestant-held La Fère in Normandy, and set out with a brother, two friends, and servants, on a fifteen-month trip (September, 1580–November, 1581) through Germany, Switzerland, and Austria to Italy. His main reasons for the trip were his health, heartsickness over France, weariness of domesticity, desire to see Venice and especially Rome, and sheer love of travel. Two years earlier, in the summer of 1578, he had contracted the acutely painful illness of the kidney stone, which had helped kill his father and which he had long feared. His experience of it had been a pleasant surprise; for, finding that life was still tolerable, he had lost his fear of pain. Still he hoped to find relief in mineral baths outside of France, seeing nothing to fear in such a natural cure. Except for a five-month sojourn in Rome, his longest stays were two, for a total of over two months, at the baths of La Villa near Lucca.

He left a record of his trip, not intended for publication and not published until 1774, in what we know as his *Journal de Voyage* (*Travel Journal*), about three hundred pages long in most editions. The first half was dictated to a secretary; the other half—of which half is in Italian—he wrote himself after dismissing his secretary in Rome. No rival to the *Essais*, the *Journal* still has much to recommend it. It gives Montaigne's readers a reassuring check on his self-portrait in the *Essais* and shows several aspects that are not wholly expected: his interest in all kinds of religious beliefs and practices and fondness for theological debate; his surprising delight in mechanical ingenuity, even gadgetry; and his friendly outgoingness toward all comers. It documents for us the frequency and acuteness of his bouts with the stone. Finally, it gives us his report (1228–29, S955–56) of the friendly reception—despite a few criticisms[5]—of his book in Rome by the official papal censor, the Master of the Sacred Palace. Though a century later (1676) the *Essais* were to be placed on the Index, in Montaigne's own time they were viewed favorably by the Church.

Montaigne was at La Villa when in September, 1581, he learned that a month before he had been elected mayor of Bordeaux—probably not because of his father's example, as he believed, but as the one man of judgment acceptable to all four princely parties most concerned: Henry III, Catherine de' Medici, Henry of Navarre, and his wife, the king's sister, Margaret of Valois. He returned expecting to decline, feeling ill and unfit for the job; but a politely firm letter from the king changed his mind. His first two-year term, which led to his re-election, was rather quiet and uneventful. Not so the second. There were strong Leaguers within the city and Protestant forces nearby. Though in writing about his term of office he stresses the freedom from passionate involvement that kept the man and the mayor always separate, the twenty letters we possess that he wrote in his second term (1583–85), mostly to his loyalist co-worker Marshal Jacques de Matignon, the king's lieutenant general in the southwest, reveal him clearly as a vigilant, hardworking, and efficient administrator. His failure—though approved by his assistants, the jurats—to return into the city, decimated by the plague, at the end of his second term for the transferal of authority to his successor Matignon (with whom he was staying nearby) has been criticized by many commentators; but to him this would have been an idle gesture, not heroism but heroics.

After a peaceful year at home with his *Essais,* Montaigne had a trying time in July, 1586, when a large League army, with the reluctant approval of the king, marched south and laid siege to Protestant-held Castillon, on the Dordogne about five miles from Montaigne. He was pillaged by soldiers camped on his land and found himself, as a moderate with friends on both sides, suspect to both warring camps. Then the plague broke out among the besiegers and spread to the doomed town and to Montaigne's estate. He had to take his family away for six months in quest of asylum before returning home (early spring of 1587) and resuming work on his book.

Part of his time was spent at the conferences at Saint-Brice near Cognac, where he was summoned by Catherine de' Medici for a hopeless attempt to persuade Henry of Navarre to abjure and return to court. Late in the same year, three days after Navarre had won the first big Protestant victory of the wars at Coutras, he paid his second overnight visit to Montaigne, who may well have been instrumental in persuading him not to follow up his advantage by a march north that threatened to lead to armed conflict with the king. Less than three months later (February, 1588) Montaigne was on his way to Paris on a secret mission sponsored by Matignon, from Henry of Navarre to Henry III, seeking to bring the two into closer alliance against the menacing League. It was the substance of the mission that was secret; the fact of it was reported with interest by both the English and Spanish ambassadors. Suspect once again to both extremist parties—to the Leaguers for obvious reasons, to the Protestants because they were being bypassed and feared another abjuration by Navarre—Montaigne was held up and detained by Protestants on the way and, that summer, imprisoned by Leaguers in the Bastille until the queen mother secured his speedy release.

He spent nearly all the year 1588 in the north, following the king in his flight from Paris to Chartres and Rouen; meeting and visiting his "covenant daughter," enthusiastic admirer, and future literary executrix, Marie de Gournay; probably seeing to the Paris publication of the first three-book edition of the *Essais;* and attending the Estates-General at Blois, where Henry III finally had Henri de Guise killed.

Around the end of that year Montaigne returned south, where he helped Matignon in keeping Bordeaux and the region loyal first to Henry III and then, after his assassination, to Henry IV. Two letters of 1590 from Montaigne to his new king—whose success he says he had hoped for even when he had to confess this to his curate—reveal that he was invited to join him, that he was ready to be the kind of firm, frank counselor he had wanted to be, and that illness and delays in the mails dashed these hopes. In his last few years he continued to work on his *Essais,* adding no new books or chapters (as he doubtless felt that time was short) but about a thousand passages that are in the main his boldest and most original. In his last two years, when illness confined him more and more to his château, he watched his life ebb with serenity. According to the best available account (we have none by an eyewitness), a quinsy rendered him speechless, able to communicate only by written notes, for his last three days. On September 13, 1592, at the age of fifty-nine, he died peacefully, hearing Mass in his room.

❧ III ❧

THE DECISION TO WRITE

Though Montaigne regards bookworms and professional men of letters with the disdain of the gentleman amateur for the pedant (I: 26, 163, S121; II: 37, 764, S596), he often acknowledges his love for books. Their companionship, always available, consoles him in old age and solitude, rescues him from boredom and from disagreeable thoughts or company, and dulls the pangs of sorrow. *"C'est la meilleure munition que j'aye trouvé à cet humain voyage."* ["It is the best provision I have found for this human journey."] (III: 3, 805–6, S628.)

He learned to love them early. At seven or eight no pleasure could lure him away from Ovid; next it was the *Æneid*, Plautus, Terence, and some Italian comedies (I: 26, 175, S130); at fifteen he owned a complete Virgil. In his thirties he read avidly in history and memoirs, leaving careful notes. His own translation of Sebond and dedicatory letters to La Boétie's works show assiduity as well as skill.

In his retirement he could not be satisfied merely to read. He would probably rather, he writes later (II: 8, 383, S293), have produced one perfect brainchild of a book than one perfect man-child. What led him to "this daydream of meddling with writing," he says, was *"une humeur melancholique, . . . produite par le chagrin de la solitude en laquelle il y a quelques années que je m'estoy jetté"* ["a melancholy humor, . . . produced by the gloom of the solitude into which I had cast myself some years ago"] (II: 8, 364, S278). In what may have been a first preface to his book (I: 8, 34, S21) he says he wanted to contemplate the vagaries of his runaway mind. When he retired, seeking rest and seclusion, he thought to favor his mind by letting it settle in itself, as he hoped it was now mature enough to do; but on the contrary,

> il . . . m'enfante tant de chimeres et monstres fantastiques les uns sur les autres, sans ordre et sans propos, que pour en contempler à mon aise l'ineptie et l'estrangeté, j'ay commancé de les mettre en rolle, esperant avec le temps luy en faire honte à luy mesmes.

> [it . . . gives birth to so many chimeras and fantastic monsters, one after another, without order or purpose, that in order to con-template their ineptitude and strangeness at my pleasure, I have begun to put them in writing, hoping in time to make my mind ashamed of itself.]

In short, he knew he had something to say and a need to write. The problem was what. As far as we can tell,[1] the plan that em-braced himself as his subject and the *Essais* as the probings of that self still lay six or seven years ahead; he was to find it only as he worked and thought his book. Meanwhile his early interests—war, history and biography, moral philosophy and the problems of life—emerge in his earliest chapters, composed between 1571 and 1573.

Many of these resemble a popular genre of the time, the *"diverses leçons"* ["varied readngs"] of such minor writers as Crinito, Aulus Gellius, Antonio de Guevara, Pedro de Mexia, and Coelius Rhodi-ginus. Short groups of anecdotes with a brief moral, they reveal little of Montaigne. A good example is I: 7, "Que l'intention juge nos actions" ["That Intention Is Judge of Our Actions"]; others are I: 5–6, 13, 15–17, 24, 34, 45. More interesting but also rather im-personal are the chapters (I: 2–4, 9–11, 18, 21, 23, 33, 36–38, 43–44, 46–48) that treat some aspect of human behavior, usually to stress some paradox of our inconsistency and frailty.

In the most interesting of these earliest chapters Montaigne con-fronts his greatest problems of these years: identity and consistency (II: 1), retirement (I: 39), and especially pain and death (I: 14; I: 19–20, etc.). Here his current attitudes are most fully expressed—the attitudes that are to change the most during the remaining twenty years of his life.

The question of change in Montaigne has been much debated. Of course he remains Montaigne in all his mature years—skeptical, tolerant, conservative, practical, a stanch Catholic, fond of life, concerned above all with how to live. As he says himself, the very knowledge of his own mobility has helped him gain a certain constancy of opinion (II: 12, 553, S428); he is nearly always in place, like inert bodies, and his firmest ideas are those he was born with (III: 2, 789, S615).

However, since he never closes his mind, some of his key attitudes do change. An early chapter, I: 20, is entitled "Que philosopher c'est apprendre à mourir" ["That to Philosophize Is to Learn to Die"]; about six years later he writes that "la philosophie est celle qui nous instruict à vivre" ["it is philosophy that teaches us to live"] (I: 26, 162, S120). In the same early chapter he states that "Le but de nostre carriere, c'est la mort, c'est l'object necessaire de nostre visée" ["The goal of our career is death. It is the necessary object of our aim"] (I: 20, 82, S57); but in his final additions nearly twenty years later, presumably with this statement in mind, he writes of death: "Mais il m'est advis que c'est bien le bout, non pourtant le but de la vie; c'est sa fin, son extremité, non pourtant son object." ["But it seems to me that death is indeed the end, but not therefore the goal, of life; it is its finish, its extremity, but not therefore its object."] (III: 12, 1028, S805.)

Likewise with pain. In one of his early chapters he writes that life offers us more to avoid than to enjoy, since the greatest well-being we can hope for is freedom from pain. He never changes this statement; but when he reads it over in his final years he adds that while he is glad to be well, if he is sick he wants to feel it; to eradicate pain would be to extirpate pleasure and annihilate man; pain is not always to be avoided, nor pleasure always to be pursued.[2]

Montaigne recognizes this element of change. This is precisely why he does not correct his first ideas by later ones; he wants to represent each idea at its birth, and wishes he had begun earlier, so that he might trace the course of his mutations (II: 37, 736–37, S574). "Je ne peints pas l'estre," he writes. "Je peints le passage. . . . Il faut accommoder mon histoire à l'heure. Je pourray tantost changer, non de fortune seulement, mais aussi d'intention." ["I do not portray being: I portray passing. . . . My history needs to be adapted to the moment. I may presently change, not only by chance, but also by intention."] (III: 2, 782, S611.) Looking back in his last years at his earliest Essais, he states: "Moy à cette heure et moy

tantost, sommes bien deux . . . " ["Myself now and myself a while
ago are indeed two . . ."] (III: 9, 941, S736.)

The earliest chapters are rarely gay. A characteristic observation
is the one just noted, that freedom from pain is the best state man
can hope for. Death seems to be the main fact of life, with pain its
accessory evil. This is not surprising: within ten years Montaigne
had lost his dearest friend, his beloved father, a young brother, and
his long-awaited first child; he had come close to death on a peaceful horseback ride; the civil wars raged all around, and St. Bartholomew's Day was close at hand. His chapter "De la solitude" ["Of
Solitude"] (I: 39) shows a firm determination to make himself so
independent of others that he cannot be hurt by their loss (I: 39,
235–36, S177–78; cf. III: 4, 814, S635).

The great enemies are pain and death. Death, our inevitable
end, has always been on Montaigne's mind; the earliest *Essais* are
full of the theme. La Boétie's example had taught Montaigne how
bravely a man could meet it and how this must be the aim of all
our studies. In I: 19 ("Qu'il ne fault juger de nostre heur qu'après
la mort" ["That Our Happiness Must Not Be Judged until after
Our Death"]) he argues that everywhere else we may play a part,
but not in death; hence that is the test of all our lives. *"Je remets à
la mort l'essay du fruict de mes estudes. Nous verrons là si mes discours me partent de la bouche, ou du cœur."* ["I leave it to death
to test the fruit of my studies. We shall see then whether my rea-
sonings come from my mouth or from my heart."] "De juger de la
mort d'autruy" ["Of Judging of the Death of Others"] (II: 13)
treats death in a similar way. Only a little later, in "De l'exercitation" ["Of Practice"] (II: 6) will Montaigne come to look at death
more relaxedly.

Montaigne's key chapter on the subject, "Que philosopher c'est
apprendre à mourir" ["That to Philosophize Is to Learn to Die"]
(I: 20), brings *apprendre* very close to its cognate *apprehend*. It is
a mosaic by a Stoically oriented but eclectic humanist—in the sixteenth-century sense of the term: a lover of the literature and wisdom of ancient Greece and Rome concerned with man, his world,
and his conduct—in which Pliny, Plutarch, and Lucretius rub el-
bows with Cicero and Seneca. Since the fear of death is the greatest

threat to human happiness, Montaigne argues, we must strive to overcome it by premeditation. Thoughtlessness is useless, a brutish stupidity that costs too dear, since it leaves us in torment when death catches us unawares. We must live and act, to be sure; but above all we must prepare.

To attack the problem of pain Montaigne examines the validity of his chapter title "Que le goust des biens et des maux depend en bonne partie de l'opinion que nous en avons" ["That the Taste of Good and Evil Depends in Large Part on the Opinion We Have of Them"] (I: 14), and finds that this holds for death but not so well for pain. Whereas our imagination can make death indifferent or even attractive to us, pain is a matter of certain knowledge and the thing we fear even in death. If it is violent, it cannot last; as a last resort there is suicide. Our main hope, however, is in the tension of the soul. *"Elle [la douleur] se rendra de bien meilleure composition à qui luy fera teste. Il se faut opposer et bander contre."* ["It [pain] will make itself far easier to deal with to those who stand up against it. We must resist it and tense ourselves against it."] (I: 14, 58, S39.)

As Montaigne sees it, the duty of the humanist noble is to meet pain and death not just adequately, but well; this is how the superior man distinguishes himself. In a way we should be grateful for pain. Unless we have it to bear with resolute calm, *"par où s'acquerra l'advantage que nous voulons avoir sur le vulgaire?"* ["how shall we acquire the advantage that we wish to have over the common herd?"] (I: 14, 56, S38.)

Another problem for Montaigne, and another distinction between the sage and the vulgar, is consistency. In "De l'inconstance de nos actions" ["Of the Inconsistency of Our Actions"] (II: 1), he finds hardly a dozen consistent lives in all antiquity and lists only one model, Cato the Younger. The rest of us, he writes, are so variable, such puppets of impulses from without and within, that *"se trouve autant de différence de nous à nous mesmes, que de nous à autruy"* ["there is as much difference between us and ourselves as between us and others"] (II: 1, 321, S244).

Even greater than this difference is that between the sage and the vulgar. Montaigne begins his chapter "De l'inequalité qui est entre nous" ["Of the Inequality That Is Between Us"] (I: 42) with another paradox: *"il y a plus de distance de tel à tel homme qu'il n'y a de tel homme à telle beste"* ["there is more distance from a given man to a given man than from a given man to a given animal"] (I: 42, 250, S189). We all tend, he notes, to measure men by their trappings, not by themselves. The true distinction between men has nothing to do with wealth or rank.

> *Si, les yeux ouverts, elle [son âme] attend les espées traites . . . si elle est rassise, equable et contente: c'est ce qu'il faut veoir, et juger par là les extremes differences qui sont entre nous . . . Un tel homme est cinq cent brasses au-dessus des Royaumes et des duchez: il est luy mesmes à soy son empire . . . Comparez à celuy là la tourbe de nos hommes, ignorante, stupide et endormie, basse, servile, pleine de fiebvre et de fraieur, instable,[3] et continuellement flotante en l'orage des passions diverses qui la poussent et tempestent, pendant toute d'autruy; il y a plus d'esloignement que du Ciel à la terre . . .* (I: 42, 252, S190–91; cf. DB I, 217–18.)
>
> [If open-eyed it [his soul] awaits the drawn swords . . . if it is composed, equable, and content: this is what we must see, and by this judge the extreme differences that are between us. . . . Such a man is five hundred fathoms above kingdoms and duchies; he is himself his own empire. . . . Compare with him the common run of men today, ignorant, stupid, and asleep, base, servile, full of fever and fright, unstable, and continually floating in the tempest of the diverse passions that drive and toss them about; depending entirely on others. There is more distance between them than between heaven and earth.]

In short, Montaigne's problem in the earliest *Essais* is not just that of meeting pain and death, but of meeting them bravely, in the manner of a noble sage, not of the vulgar. His solution seeks arms against a sea of troubles in books, in the sages, in self-mastery by reason and will. Stoical in coloration, it is nonetheless eclectic. It is perhaps best described as that of an apprehensive humanist.

⋘ IV ⋙

SKEPTICISM:
TEMPER AND TOOL

The chapters composed in the next few years (1573–75) show Montaigne experimenting with structure, glimpsing what his project is to be, and reassessing certain attitudes and values. He begins "De l'yvrongnerie" ["Of Drunkenness"] (II: 2) with a rather severe condemnation of that vice, then goes on, as if saying "but, come to think of it," to point to illustrious examples that tone down his rigor. The next chapter, "Coustume de l'isle de Cea" ["A Custom of the Island of Cea"] (II: 3), provides a real turnabout: after two pages in praise of suicide and its benefits, Montaigne turns abruptly to the various arguments that condemn it—only to make at least an apparent turn again and examine situations in which it may be permissible. In "De l'exercitation" ["Of Practice"] (II: 6) he builds an entire chapter and a modified view of death on an accident he had on horseback, which he relates at length; and the original version of the chapter ends (II: 6, 357, S272) with a statement that foreshadows self-study and the essay plan. And it was probably during these years that Montaigne wrote one or more substantial treatments of human vanity that were to be parts of the book-length "Apologie de Raimond Sebond" ["Apology for Raymond Sebond"] (II: 12).

As he reflects on his earliest message of tension and premeditation, he seems to wonder whether his life can be that of the humanist sage, of a La Boétie or a Cato. From the first he had noted how much he differs from some of his heroes (I: 37, 225, S169). He knows that what we want to be is limited by what we are, since we cannot wholeheartedly wish to change much: *"C'est de pareille vanité que nous desirons estre autre chose que ce que nous sommes. Le fruict d'un tel desir ne nous touche pas, d'autant qu'il se con-*

tredict et s'empesche en soy." ["It is by a similar vanity that we wish to be something other than we are. The object of such a desire does not really affect us, inasmuch as the desire contradicts and hinders itself within."] (II: 3, 334, S254.) And nothing can be useful to us unless it is wholly ours: *"Quand bien nous pourrions estre sçavans du sçavoir d'autruy, au moins sages ne pouvons nous estre que de nostre propre sagesse."* ["Even if we could be learned with other men's learning, at least wise we cannot be except with our own wisdom."] (I: 25, 137, S101.)

Even in his earliest chapters Montaigne had shown chinks in the armor of Stoical humanism. The proud refusal of the Stoic Posidonius to call the pain that gripped him an evil strikes him as comically histrionic (I: 14, 55, S37). Seneca's advice to abandon either his life of pomp and pleasure or life itself, though actually borrowed from Epicurus, sounds to him like Stoical harshness, which he sharply contrasts with Christian moderation (I: 33, 216, S162).

Finding that Stoical humanism ignores or seeks to suppress certain facts of human nature (I: 39, 237, S179), Montaigne soon comes to consider it impractical and unsound. The consistency he had sought in it he now finds incompatible precisely with the heroic actions he had most admired:

Quand nous arrivons à ces saillies Stoïques: "J'ayme mieux estre furieux que voluptueux" . . . quand Epicurus . . . deffie les maux, et, mesprisant les douleurs moins aspres, . . . en appelle et desire des fortes, poignantes et dignes de luy . . . qui ne juge que ce sont boutées d'un courage eslancé hors de son giste? . . . Aristote . . . a raison d'appeler folie tout eslancement, tant löuable soit-il, qui surpasse nostre propre jugement et discours. D'autant que la sagesse c'est un maniment reglé de nostre ame, et qu'elle conduit avec mesure et proportion, et s'en respond. (II: 2, 329–30, S251.)

[When we come to such Stoical sallies as *I would rather be insane than voluptuous* . . . when Epicurus . . . defies ills, and, scorning the less severe pains . . . invokes and wishes for pains strong, biting, and worthy of him . . . who does not judge that these are the sallies of a courage flung out of its abode? . . . Aristotle . . . is right to call madness any transport, however laudable, that transcends our own judgment and reason; inasmuch as wisdom is an orderly management of our soul, which she conducts with measure and proportion and is responsible for.]

In the same chapter ("Of Drunkenness") Montaigne greets with a snort of derision the "old and amusing question" whether wine can overcome the soul of the sage. What conceited creatures we are! he comments. Not one soul in a thousand is straight and composed for even one moment in a lifetime; to combine this with constancy is perfection itself: *"Tant sage qu'il voudra, mais en fin c'est un homme: qu'est il plus caduque, plus miserable et plus de neant? La sagesse ne force pas nos conditions naturelles . . ."* ["For all his wisdom, the sage is still a man: what is there more vulnerable, more wretched, and more null? Wisdom does not overcome our natural limitations . . ."] (II: 2, 327–28, S249.)

The Stoics had recommended a timely suicide for the sage, and made much of this as man's unalienable right and ultimate resource against the ills of life. Montaigne begins his treatment of this subject, in "A Custom of the Island of Cea" (II: 3), by rehearsing arguments of this sort. Then, however, with the statement *"Cecy ne s'en va pas sans contraste"* ["This does not pass without contradiction"], he turns to the various condemnations of suicide. God alone, says the Christian, has the right to remove us from our post here below. Suicide, however you look at it, is a cowardly way of hiding under a massive tomb to escape the blows of fortune. And insofar as it shows contempt for life, it is ridiculous and sickly.

> *Et l'opinion qui desdaigne nostre vie, elle est ridicule en nous, car en fin c'est nostre estre, c'est nostre tout . . . C'est une maladie particuliere, et qui ne se voit en nulle autre creature, de se hayr et de se combattre.* (II: 3, 334, S254; cf. DB I, 289.)
>
> [And the opinion that disdains our life is ridiculous in us. For after all it is our being, it is our all. . . . It is a malady peculiar to man, and not seen in any other creature, to hate and combat himself.]

In short, in the essays of 1573–75 Montaigne often attacks certain aspects of Stoical humanism—especially its heroic extremes—as unfit for himself (and possibly for most men), comically histrionic, inconsistent, presumptuous, un-Christian, cowardly, and unnatural. He is well on his way to his next step, which will fill the "Apology for Raymond Sebond": a devastating critique of all dogmatic philosophy.

The "Apology" is the central statement of Montaigne's most famous attribute, his skepticism. This is the chapter which appeared to Sainte-Beuve, writing of Montaigne in his *Port-Royal*, as the perfidious core of the *Essais*; which prompted Emerson to represent him as "Montaigne; or, the Skeptic" among his *Representative Men*, and T. S. Eliot to grant him a dangerous greatness for managing to express the skepticism of every man. But to call a man a skeptic is merely to begin a statement, not to complete one.

Montaigne's skepticism is used not to cast doubt on Catholicism but to support it by placing it beyond the reach of reason. His is the position of the fideist, who humbles reason in religious matters to the advantage of faith.

In Montaigne's skepticism it is useful to distinguish between temper and tool: between the natural reaction of his whole mind, if not his whole being, to multiplicity and flux, and the doctrinal, systematic theory of human uncertainty that he sometimes uses—as in the "Apology"—to convict us of ignorance and humble our presumption.

Montaigne's intellectual temper was probably always skeptical. In the etymological sense of the term, he is one who stops for a good look before any mental leap, who considers all sides before choosing his own. Since nature, as he sees it, has made things more unlike than like, all comparisons are lame and all statements oversimplifications. He never forgets that even the soundest views of his milieu and moment—or of any other—may be far from absolute truths. His acute sense of flux, the law of the world we live in, makes him doubt that anything as constant and enduring as absolute truth can dwell in us—or, if by chance it can, that we can know it.

Skepticism in its systematic or doctrinal form is found mainly in the "Apology." In a sense it is everywhere; for classical skepticism accepts customs, laws, and natural feelings as guides in life, and experience and appearances as matters not subject to doubt.[1] But Montaigne is too concerned with action to be always a patient doubter; he tends to follow common sense and accept appearances as facts. Thus he can criticize Pyrrhonism once as an ingenious way of using reason to undermine experience, and again as an amusing science built of ignorance (see pp. 29–30).

The "Apology for Raymond Sebond" is a puzzling chapter, because it is hardly a defense at all. Virtually every reference to

Sebond is apologetic; Montaigne is at pains to dissociate himself from him. Everything about his translation of the *Natural Theology* seems to have occurred by chance or by command: some days before his death, his father came across the book by chance in a pile of other abandoned papers and commanded Michel to put it into French; Michel happened to be at leisure and could not disobey the best father that ever was; so he got through it as best he could; his father was pleased and ordered it to be printed (II: 12, 415–16, S319–20). When Montaigne uses a possessive about Sebond and his book, it is never first person: referring to the ladies, he speaks of it as "their book" (417, S320); and addressing Margaret of Valois, speaks of him as "your Sebond" (540, S418). He manages, in his opening pages, to say a few nice things about Sebond; but most of these are extremely guarded, like the following summary of the value of the book:

> La foy venant à teindre et illustrer les argumens de Sebond, elle les rend fermes et solides; ils sont capables de servir d'acheminement et de premiere guyde à un aprentis pour le mettre à la voye de cette connoissance . . . (II: 12, 425, S327.)
>
> [Faith, coming to color and illumine Sebond's arguments, makes them firm and solid; they are capable of serving as a start and a first guide to an apprentice to set him on the road to this knowledge . . .]

There is irony here as well as lavish qualification; for whereas Sebond's aim is to prove his points without recourse to faith, it is his faith that makes his arguments strong.

The proportions of the "Apology" show how small a place Sebond holds in it. In the Dezeimeris and Barckhausen edition that reproduces its original version, the chapter occupies 170 pages. After a three-page introduction, Montaigne discusses and seeks to answer two objections made to Sebond's book. On the first objection and reply, he spends seven pages; on the second objection, barely a page. The remaining 159 pages, well over ninety per cent of the chapter, are a counterattack launched against the second group of critics of Sebond but involving all dogmatic philosophers, especially the ancients; and the conclusion of the chapter is a conclusion to this counterattack.

Not only is Sebond largely forgotten in the chapter; as a rationalist and a dogmatist, he implicitly suffers from Montaigne's counter-attack, especially in two areas. When Montaigne asks what can be more vain than to try to divine God by our analogies and conjectures,[2] he is talking about precisely what Sebond does. And his long parallel between man and the animals goes directly against Sebond's whole demonstration of our superiority over the rest of creation.[3] In short, as one critic has aptly put it, Montaigne supports Sebond as the rope supports the hanged man.[4]

This is why many critics, such as Sainte-Beuve, have seen the "Apology" as a perfidious attack on Sebond and indeed on Christianity itself. Yet this view is hard to accept. Montaigne is constantly concerned with being sincere; his whole life bespeaks his stanch Catholicism; if he is perfidious here, he must be a thoroughgoing dissembler. His religious views were acceptable in his own time, drawing no serious criticism from the official papal censor. He could hardly know that later admirers would apply his critique of other religions to Catholicism, which he had tried to set above the reach of reason; or that a hundred years later (1676) the *Essais* would be placed on the Index of Prohibited Books.

Nor is it much easier to believe, as some of Montaigne's defenders have argued, that he simply forgot about Sebond throughout most of a chapter written expressly to defend him.

A third explanation is more likely. The main statements of Montaigne's Pyrrhonism in the "Apology" probably date from around 1576; parts of the chapter seem likely to have been composed as early as 1573. About two-thirds of the way through the chapter Montaigne pauses to address a very noble lady (he speaks of "your courts") for whom he says he has extended this piece beyond his wont, and urges her to defend "your Sebond" with the ordinary arguments in which she is daily instructed, using the following part of the chapter only with the greatest caution and if "one of these new doctors" tries to be ingenious in her presence at the risk of his salvation and her own (II: 12, 540–42, S418–20). The lady in question is clearly Margaret of Valois, Catholic sister of Henry III and wife of the Protestant Navarre. She knew Montaigne and had read Sebond, presumably in Montaigne's translation. In the autumn of 1578 she joined her husband in Gascony and found herself surrounded by Protestant ministers eager to convert her. In all probability she asked Montaigne, late in 1578 or in 1579, to write a defense of the author he had translated.

Thus the theory that seems to account best for the problems of the "Apology" is that most of it was composed without Sebond in mind at all, before Montaigne was asked to defend him. He was clearly no great admirer of the Spaniard, whom he considered useful —in a limited way—but rather weak.[5] However, Sebond was on the right side; his chief critics were just the kind of arrogant dogmatists against whom Montaigne had already written with some relish. Bidden by a beleaguered Catholic queen to give a command performance on Sebond's behalf, Montaigne probably decided that he could set his fragments into a framework that would make of them an "Apology for Raymond Sebond."

The "Apology" as Montaigne finally put it together for publication in 1580 may be divided (again using the pagination of the Dezeimeris and Barckhausen edition to show the original proportions) into six unequal parts of which three (numbers 2, 3, and 5) constitute almost nine-tenths of the chapter.

Part 1 (15 pages) is a brief introduction telling about the book and how Montaigne came to translate it, stating the two objections, commenting on the first, and preparing for the counterattack against the second group of critics of Sebond.

Part 2 is a 58-page collection of stories showing that animals are just as intelligent and generally admirable as man, and furthermore (for the last 16 pages) that if man does have some distinguishing faculty of reason, this makes him neither happy nor good.

Part 3 (46 pages) is a demonstration that man knows nothing (and thus that skepticism is the only human wisdom), by pointing out his ignorance of God or the gods, of himself in general, of his own soul or reason, and of his body.

Part 4 is a two-page warning to the princess (the unnamed Queen Margaret) that what will follow is a dangerous fencer's trick, to be used only as a last resort, by which you abandon your own weapon (reason) to make your adversary lose his.

Part 5 (48 pages) is an argument that man can have no knowledge, or know that he has it if by chance he has; this largely because man is a creature of flux, who can know neither flux nor being, and because all his instruments of knowledge, notably the senses, are demonstrably deficient and deceptive.

Part 6 is a one-page conclusion praising Seneca's feeling that man must raise himself above humanity but pronouncing it absurd, since God alone, by his grace, can work such a miracle.

No further details should be needed to show that the dominant theme of the "Apology" is Pyrrhonistic skepticism. Yet insofar as this position is a statement (or a question) about human knowledge, there are curious things about it here. There is much in the chapter that tempers Montaigne's famous one-time motto "*Que sçay-je?*" ["What do I know?"] (II: 12, 508, S393.)

For one thing, Montaigne can be critical of Pyrrhonism, as when he tells the story of the innovation-monger who insisted that the ancients were all wrong about the winds. When Montaigne pointed out that they seemed to get where they set out for, the man replied that they were simply lucky and still wrong. Montaigne goes on:

> *Je luy repliquay lors que j'aymois mieux suyvre les effets que la raison.*
>
> *Or ce sont choses qui se choquent souvent . . . et les Pyrrhoniens ne se servent de leurs argumens et de leur raison que pour ruiner l'apparence de l'experience; et est merveille jusques où la souplesse de nostre raison les a suivis à ce dessein de combattre l'evidence des effects . . .* (II: 12, 554–55, S430.)

> [I then replied to him that I would rather follow facts than reason.
>
> Now these are things that often clash . . . And the Pyrrhonians use their arguments and their reason only to ruin the apparent facts of experience; and it is marvelous how far the suppleness of our reason has followed them in this plan of combating the evidence of the facts.]

Three other chapters of Book II, all composed presumably soon after most of the "Apology," contain remarks that contrast with some of its skeptical themes. At the very end of the preceding chapter (II: 11, 414, S317–18) Montaigne writes quite detachedly about the parallel between man and the animals. Elsewhere he states (II: 8, 366, S279) that since God has given us a certain capacity for reason so that we are not, like the animals, enslaved to the common laws, we must not let nature tyrannize us but be guided

in our inclinations by reason alone. Whereas in the "Apology" he
had rejected some comical stories about Pyrrho, elsewhere he accepts
them and describes him as "the one who built such an amusing
science out of ignorance" (II: 29, 683–84, S533).

Within the "Apology" there are clear limits to his attack. It is
our claims to know what we cannot know that are his targets.
Much of experience, especially experience of self, emerges virtually
unscathed; and he draws from it many of his demonstrations of
our changes, illusions, and intellectual frailty. The "Apology" re-
peatedly raises the question: If we cannot know ourselves, what
can we know? (II: 12, 543, S421; cf. 523, S405.) Montaigne's answer
is clear from the first: that we can know something about ourselves, and that for us this is the beginning of wisdom as well as
of knowledge (II: 12, 545–54, S423–30).

A large part of the appeal of Pyrrhonism to Montaigne in the
"Apology" is as a way of life. He is critical now of Stoical humanism, but he has not yet fully discovered his ultimate master Socrates.
In rejecting now the legend which he was to accept later, of Pyrrho
as an unsociable anarchist needing to be saved by his friends from
carts and precipices, he writes of him and his followers in this way:

*Quant aux actions de la vie, ils [les Pyrrhoniens] sont en cela de
la commune façon. Ils se prestent et accommodent aux inclinations
naturelles, à l'impulsion et contrainte des passions, aux constitutions
des loix et des coustumes et à la tradition des arts . . . sans aucune
opination ou jugement. . . . Pyrrho . . . n'a pas voulu se faire
pierre ou souche; il a voulu se faire homme vivant, discourant et
raisonnant, jouissant de tous plaisirs et commoditez naturelles, em-
besoignant et se servant de toutes ses pieces corporelles et spirituelles.
Les privileges fantastiques, imaginaires et faux que l'homme s'est
usurpé, de juger, de connoistre, de sçavoir, d'ordonner, d'establir,
il les a de bonne foy renoncez et quittez.* (II: 12, 485–86, S374; cf.
DB II, 95.)

[As for the actions of life, they [the Pyrrhonists] are of the common
fashion in that. They lend and accommodate themselves to natural
inclinations, to the impulsion and constraint of passions, to the
constitutions of laws and customs, and to the tradition of the arts
. . . without any taking sides or judgment. . . . Pyrrho . . . did not
want to make himself a stump or a stone; he wanted to make himself a living, thinking, reasoning man, enjoying all natural pleasures
and comforts, employing and using all his bodily and spiritual

faculties. The fantastic, imaginary, false privileges that man has
arrogated to himself, of judging, knowing, ordering, and establishing,
he honestly renounced and gave up.]

Pyrrhonism for Montaigne is also a method and a tool. The
irresponsible way in which he says its followers argue, not caring
who wins so long as dogmatic belief is shaken (II: 12, 483, S372),
applies to much of his own argument in this chapter, but not elsewhere. He uses it as a weapon to attack two favorite groups of
adversaries: the Protestant and rationalist critics of Sebond, and
their ancestors in pride of knowledge, the ancient dogmatic philosophers.

Already critical of Stoical humanism before the "Apology," by
the end of his work on this chapter Montaigne has finished with
it. Man, he now finds, is a presumptuous animal, no wiser, happier,
or better than his fellow creatures. His premeditation of troubles
is less helpful than simple acceptance of life as it comes. Dogmatic
philosophy is presumptuous, absurd, and an obstacle to Christian
faith; only Pyrrhonism is wise in itself and a sound basis for
Christianity. Stoical humanism, ignoring man's condition, seeks in
vain to raise him above it; God alone can do that.

What is left for us as creatures of flux incapable of true knowledge? To learn the lesson of flux, to become "wise at our own
expense" (II: 12, 546, S423) by knowing ourselves.

That is the task, now already started, that lies ahead for
Montaigne. The "Apology" is among other things a declaration of
intellectual independence. His former heroes and teachers, the
Stoical humanists, have been exposed and abandoned as inadequate.
Now he is free of their tutelage and ready to look within himself
for instruction and guidance.

❧ V ☙

THE SUBJECT AS SELF:
THE ESSAY

The last few years before the first *Essais* (Books I–II) appeared in 1580 were very productive. Besides bringing together the parts of his "Apology for Raymond Sebond," Montaigne composed about thirty new chapters (I: 26, 31; II: 7–11, 16–37) which include some of his best—those on education (I: 26), cannibals (I: 31), the affection of fathers for their children (II: 8), books (II: 10), cruelty (II: 11), glory (II: 16), presumption (II: 17), giving the lie (II: 18), and the resemblance of children to fathers (II: 37). These constitute about one-third of the first two books, and show a greater freedom of association than before. His productivity is natural; for it is now that he finds his true subject—himself—and his method—the essays—and exploits them with the joy of discovery.

Self-study was, of course, no invention of Montaigne's. The temple of Apollo at Delphi, the life and thought of Socrates, had made "Know thyself" a byword among the Greeks. Sebond had stressed its necessity. Less normative, more inquiring than most of his predecessors, Montaigne had given a foretaste of his plan already in "Practice," where he concludes as follows his account of a fall from a horse after a collision:

> *Ce conte d'un evenement si legier est assez vain, n'estoit l'instruction que j'en ay tirée pour moy . . . Or, comme dict Pline, chacun est à soy-mesmes une très-bonne discipline, pourveu qu'il ait la suffisance de s'espier de près. Ce n'est pas icy ma doctrine, c'est mon estude; et n'est pas la leçon d'autruy, c'est la mienne.* (II: 6, 357, S272.)

> [This account of so trivial an event would be rather pointless, were it not for the instruction that I have derived from it for myself . . . Now as Pliny says, each man is a very good education to himself, provided he has the capacity to spy on himself from close up.

This is not my teaching, this is my study; and it is not a lesson for others, it is for me.]

It is the "Apology" that paves the way for self-study as a major theme. Montaigne ridicules the critics of Sebond who think they know everything and do not even know themselves (II: 12, 520, S402), since if man can know anything at all, it must be the thing closest and most accessible, himself (II: 12, 543, S421; cf. 523, S405). Already self-study has taught him the lesson of flux: *"Moy qui m'espie de plus prèz, qui ay les yeux incessamment tendus sur moy, comme celuy qui n'ay pas fort à-faire ailleurs . . . à peine oseroy-je dire la vanité et la foiblesse que je trouve chez moy."* ["I who spy on myself more closely, who have my eyes unceasingly intent on myself, as one who has not much business elsewhere . . . I would hardly dare tell of the vanity and weakness that I find in myself."] (II: 12, 548, S425.)

From self-study to self-portrayal can be a big step; for Montaigne apparently it was not. We have already noted his derogatory account of how solitude, then melancholy, led him to the "wild and monstrous plan" of making himself his theme and subject. He might have put it more candidly as follows: Wanting to write, I began to do so on whatever came to mind. Gradually I recognized that my one real theme was myself. I had much to say about man's vanity and frailty, but also about his resources. Studying our limitations, I became convinced that the first step toward knowledge and wisdom is self-study. I resolved to make this my vocation and to take myself as the subject of my book.

What he mainly requires of his portrait is that it be true to life. This applies to language (II: 17, 621, S483; cf. DB II, 218), to order (II: 10, 388, S297), and to style in general; each must represent Montaigne as he is. The portrait must change as the subject changes (I: 26, 147, S109; II: 37, 737, S574). Montaigne's ideas may not be true; his account of them must be (II: 10, 387, 389, S296, 298; cf. DB I, 340, 342). Handsome or ugly, his likeness must be faithful: *"Quelles que soyent ces inepties, je n'ay pas deliberé de les cacher, non plus qu'un mien pourtraict chauve et grisonnant, où le peintre auroit mis non un visage parfaict, mais le mien."* ["Whatever these absurdities may be, I have had no intention of concealing them, any more than I would a bald and graying portrait of myself, in which the painter had drawn not a perfect face, but mine."] (I: 26, 147, S108.) Or, as he writes in his note to the reader: *"Je veus qu'on m'y voie en ma façon simple, naturelle et ordinaire, sans contention et artifice: car c'est moy que je peins."* ["I want to be seen here in my simple, natural, ordinary fashion, without straining or artifice; for it is myself that I portray."] ("Au lecteur," 9, S2.)

The method Montaigne created for his self-portrait is that of essays—trials, probings, or occasional samplings of the self he was examining and of the judgment he used to examine it. He seems to have developed the plan about 1578; although his best account of it before 1580 (I: 50) cannot be dated, all the others are of 1578 or later. Both title and plan are new, though soon to be popular.

Already Montaigne, without using the noun *essais* about his plan, had often talked of *essayer* in the sense of "to test by experience." There are four instances in "Practice" (II: 6) including these two: *"Quant à la mort, nous ne la pouvons essayer qu'une fois"* ["As for death, we can try it only once"] and *"Il me semble toutefois qu'il y a quelque façon de nous apprivoiser à elle [la mort] et de l'essayer aucunement. Nous en pouvons avoir experience . . ."* ["It seems to me, however, that there is a certain way of familiarizing ourselves with death and trying it out to some extent. We can have an experience of it . . ."][1] In a sense the whole chapter is not only Montaigne's account of an *essai* of death, but also an *essai* of Montaigne himself facing death. And when he notes in conclusion that his work is an education to him, a lesson not for others but for himself, he shows that this essaying of his is a way of learning to live.

When he uses the noun *essais* in his 1580 edition, it is to designate not a genre but a procedure for exploring and revealing the self: a casual, unmethodical testing of his judgment and other natural faculties on whatever comes to mind, since every action serves to reveal us.[2]

> *Le jugement est un util à tous subjects, et se mesle par tout. A cette cause, aux essais que j'en fay icy, j'y employe toute sorte d'occasion. Si c'est un subject que je n'entende point, à cela mesme je l'essaie . . . Tantost, à un subject vain et de neant, j'essaye voir s'il trouvera dequoy luy donner corps, et dequoy l'appuier et estançonner. Tantost je le promene à un subject noble et fort tracassé, auquel il n'a rien à trouver de soy mesme . . . Là il fait*

son jeu à trier la route qui luy semble la meilleure . . . Au de-
meurant, je laisse la fortune me fournir elle mesme les sujectz,
d'autant qu'ilz me sont egalement bons; et si n'entreprans pas de les
traiter entiers et à fons de cuve. De mille visages qu'ils ont chacun,
j'en prans celuy qu'il me plait. . . . J'en trieroy bien de plus riches
et plains, si j'avoy quelque autre fin proposée que celle que j'ay.

Toute action est propre à nous faire connoistre . . . (I: 50, 289–90,
S219; cf. DB I, 252–53.)

[Judgment is a tool to use on all subjects, and comes in everywhere.
Therefore in the tests that I am making of it here, I use every
sort of occasion. If it is a subject that I do not understand at all,
even on that I essay it . . . Sometimes in a vain and nonexistent
subject I try to see if it will find the wherewithal to give it body,
prop it up, and support it. Sometimes I lead it to a noble and well-
worn subject in which it has nothing original to discover . . . There
it plays its part by choosing the way that seems best to it . . . For
the rest, I let fortune itself furnish me with subjects, since they are
all equally good to me; and moreover I do not undertake to treat
them completely and to the bottom of the vat. Of a thousand aspects
that they each have, I take the one I please. . . . I would certainly
pick out richer and fuller subjects, if I had any other purpose set
than the one I have.

Every action is fit to make us known.]

As Montaigne makes free association his ordering principle, he
takes his time in coming to the point (I: 26, 31, 50; II: 17, 37, etc.),
and his chapters grow richer and freer. We shall examine some of
these in some detail in Chapter IX. While Montaigne has not yet
found the full freedom of Book III, he is well on his way.

He is not yet ready to pronounce his self-portrait a portrait of
mankind, but the elements of such a claim are present in "Presumption" (II: 17). There he soon states (617, S481) that the subject
of his study is man; and the self-portrait that follows shows him
to be completely ordinary except for his one ability, judgment[3]—
in other words, a representative specimen to be studied, but pos-
sessed of the one faculty needed for impartial self-assessment.

Whenever he speaks of his project in these years just before
publication, he speaks disparagingly, presenting it as a "stupid
enterprise," "a wild and monstrous plan," and his essays as "inept
and trivial remarks," "absurdities," and "stupidities."[4] These remarks apply only to self-portrayal, never to self-study, which he
defends stoutly in "Presumption" (II: 17, 614–15, S478–79). More-

over, in context they are less disparaging than they might be; for often (e.g., I: 26, 146–47, S108) they contrast his book with those, full of borrowed learning but empty of self, that Montaigne finds popular but inept, the kind of book that he has no wish to write. Nonetheless, he seems convinced that his prospective readers are so sure to brand his self-scrutiny as self-love that in order to be accepted as truthful he must be less truthful than modest.

A striking novelty in the *Essais* of 1578–80 is their optimism, of which several causes are apparent. At first Montaigne seems to have accepted Seneca's argument that we can enjoy nothing which we fear to lose. Around 1576, however, he questions it, apparently for the first time, and finds that on the contrary, security in enjoyment breeds boredom (II: 15, 596–97, S463–64). Thus the precariousness of our lot now appears as no longer an obstacle to our happiness but a necessary condition of it.

In his earliest chapters, when Montaigne discussed the relation of body and soul, he seemed to place his reliance on the body (I: 39, 241, S182). Now it is the soul that he finds the stronger; it must rally to the body, control it, advise it, set it straight, in short be a husband to it (II: 17, 622–23, S484–85; cf. DB II: 220). And it is some time in the years between 1576 and 1588 that Montaigne, who in the "Apology" had noted the arbitrariness of the soul as a major proof of our ignorance, comes to see it as a virtual guarantee of our ability to be happy if we choose.[5]

Montaigne's declaration of independence in the "Apology" had been a purely intellectual step; his new method and resources had not been tested. The test came in 1578 with the agonizing pain of the kidney stone.

Until he was around forty his health was excellent (II: 6, 352, S268); for the next five years he suffered some from the kidneys, but not much. Of all afflictions he had feared the stone most. His father had got it at sixty-six and died seven years later in great pain; Michel knew he might fall heir to it (II: 37, 742, S578–79). He quoted Pliny's statement that this is the worst of three diseases that have often led to suicide (II: 3, 336, S256; cf. DB I, 291).

After a year and a half with the kidney stone, only temporary relief from two visits to mineral baths, and five or six long, painful bouts of what he calls the most sudden, painful, hopeless, and fatal of diseases, in the winter of 1579–80 Montaigne assesses the result early in the last chapter of Book II, "Of the Resemblance of Children to Fathers" (II: 37, 736–41, S574–78). Experience has taught him that his fear was much worse than the pain itself and thus confirmed his belief that most of the faculties of our soul trouble our repose more than they benefit it. Now he feels that he has taken the measure of pain.

Knowing now that he can endure, even enjoy a life marked by pain, he not only decries premeditation but makes fun of Stoical humanism for its histrionic insistence on the stiff upper lip. Why, he asks, should philosophy, whose province is reality and actions, waste its time on these vain appearances, as though it were training actors for a play? Enough for it to keep the soul firm and serene while the body is in agony; we have trouble enough with the pain without adding fresh trouble by our reason. And in all this Montaigne is not making excuses for himself; to his joy he has found that he can endure the pain like a sage or, perhaps better yet, like a man.

As his life alternates between pain and painlessness, Montaigne comes to see the two as interdependent and life as a harmony of pain and pleasure. Despite his affliction, he finds himself far better off than countless healthy men. Never has his confidence in life been so great; never again will he lose it.

He has not forgotten our limitations, but now he is ready to show our great resources. Philosophy, he now reveals, is not the prevalent counterfeit that he had ridiculed in the "Apology," but a lovely open road leading to wisdom and happiness. Where once to philosophize had meant learning to die, now it is philosophy that teaches us to live (I: 26, 159–62, S118–20; cf. DB I, 114–15).

Montaigne had rejected the philosophy of tension mainly because he came to find it artificial and unnatural: setting man apart from nature, ordering him to suppress natural impulses, and wrongly assuming that he could do so. Now he goes further, and rejects "art" in the interests of following nature. He never defines these terms, but the reader may piece together his meaning. Natural to us is whatever we share with our fellow creatures and in general whatever makes us happy: the body, most emotions, the necessary appetites, common sense, and judgment. Unnatural, or at least subject to unnatural use, are imagination, unbridled reasoning, and their noxious offspring: presumption, ambition, insatiability, apprehension, and anxiety. Montaigne's arguments in the "Apology" for nature against art had been paradoxical and sweeping. Now they become fuller and more solid; and as his confidence reaches out to all mankind, he abandons animal models for natural men.

The chapter "Of Cannibals" (I: 31) describes a tribe encountered by the French in Brazil in 1557, about whom Montaigne had learned a good deal at first and second hand. His main theme is that civilized barbarity is far worse than theirs, judicial torture than their cannibalism. They are barbarous, he says, in that they are ruled by nature and little corrupted by our art. *"Ce n'est pas raison que l'art gaigne le point d'honneur sur nostre grande et puissante mere nature. . . . Par tout où sa pureté reluit, elle fait une merveilleuse honte à nos vaines et frivoles entreprinses."* ["It is not reasonable that art should win the place of honor over our great and powerful mother nature. . . . Wherever her purity shines forth, she wonderfully puts to shame our vain and frivolous attempts."] (I: 31, 203, S152.)

The dominant trait of Montaigne's cannibals is their filial obedience to nature. Content to accept her bounty and satisfy their real needs, they lack nothing, not even *"cette grande partie, de sçavoir heureusement jouyr de leur condition et s'en contenter"* ["that great thing, the knowledge of how to enjoy their condition happily and be content with it"] (I: 31, 209, S156). No slaves to instinct and custom, they are capable of reasoning and judgment. But alas for them, Montaigne concludes ironically (213, S159), they don't wear breeches.

Montaigne uses the cannibals in his greeting to the reader to symbolize the natural candor he wants for his self-portrait. Had he been living among them, he says, in the sweet freedom of nature's first laws, *"je t'asseure que je m'y fusse très-volontiers peint tout entier, et tout nud."* ["I assure you I should very gladly have portrayed myself here entire and wholly naked."] ("Au lecteur," 9, S2.)

Now, however, Montaigne is ready to recognize something in man that sets him above the rest of creation. Having shown the dangers of reason wrongly used, he now states its value and proper use:

> Puisqu'il a pleu à Dieu nous estrener de quelque capacité de discours, affin que, comme les bestes, nous ne fussions pas servilement assujectis aux loix communes, ains que nous nous y appliquassions par jugement et liberté volontaire, nous devons bien prester un peu à la simple authorité de nature, mais non pas nous laisser tyranniquement emporter à elle; la seule raison doit avoir la conduite de nos inclinations. (II: 8, 366, S279; cf. DB I, 319.)
>
> [Since it has pleased God to give us some capacity for reason, so that we should not be, like the animals, slavishly subjected to the common laws, but should apply ourselves to them by judgment and voluntary liberty, we must indeed lend a little to the simple authority of Nature, but not let ourselves be carried away tyrannically by her; reason alone must have the guidance of our inclinations.]

In short, man has it in him to improve on nature; and the problem is not simply nature versus art, but human nature versus misguided human art. Behavior appears on three levels: natural simplicity, art or artificiality, and a higher human naturalness that is beyond art. In these matters Montaigne likes to stress the meeting of extremes. Thus, although for different reasons and in different ways, stupidity and wisdom meet in their ability to withstand the accidents of human life, which the middle ground feels but cannot endure (I: 54, 298–99, S226).

Montaigne's fullest treatment of this theme appears in "Cruelty" (II: 11), where he distinguishes two levels: virtue, which requires difficulty and struggle, and simple goodness or innocence. But then, he asks, how are we to classify Socrates, who could not even be tempted to vice, or Cato the Younger, who enjoyed virtuous action as a pleasurable test of strength? Their virtue is obviously far above that of struggle.

Though all this seems clear enough, there are curious things about Montaigne's presentation. God is on the "lowest" level, for His goodness is effortless. Cato in many ways seems close to the middle one, and Montaigne clearly sets his power below the ease of Socrates. Montaigne himself is, of course, on the bottom; but his account of such effort as he has made to control his vices seems to place him nearer the top than he is willing to claim. In many ways the levels appear to represent nature, art, and perfected human nature.

From 1578 on it is this last that Montaigne takes as his ideal. By reason and judgment man can resist enslavement to natural law, train his natural faculties, and raise himself above mere nature.

Montaigne's early remarks about man are generally disparaging. Though he is no misanthrope, the spectacle of human cockiness often makes him sound like one. Now he writes about this attitude with detachment, saying simply that his favorite ancient opinions about man are those that humiliate us most (II: 17, 617, S480). Having fully exposed a vast range of human limitations, he is ready to turn to our capacities. His early chapter on education, "Du pedantisme" ["Of Pedantry"] (I: 25), had been mainly a negative critique of current aims and values; now, in "The Education of Children" (I: 26), he shows what good training can do. The key faculty is judgment; its formation by practice is the aim of education. Philosophy and virtue both lead pleasantly to happiness and wisdom. Judging everything for himself, the pupil will learn to love virtue and hate vice for themselves, not from impotence or fear, and become not a book-laden donkey but a morally independent man. Judgment properly trained can make man free, versatile, wise, and happy.

In the *Essais* of 1580 Montaigne states or suggests virtually all his final ideas but one—the unity and solidarity of man. He has often assumed this but never affirmed it. In the world and in man what strikes him most is diversity. Some men, he had written (I: 42, 250, S189) are more different from some other men than from some animals. With the theme of diversity the *Essais* of 1580 begin and end. Montaigne's first chapter (I: 1, 13, S5) describes man as *"un subject merveilleusement vain, divers et ondoyant"* ["a marvelously vain, diverse, and undulating object"] on which it is hard to base any constant and uniform judgment. Book II begins with "The Inconsistency of Our Actions," which shows that we are as different from ourselves as from others (II: 1, 321, S244), and ends with the infinite diversity of human opinions: *"Et, à l'advanture, ne fut il jamais au monde deux opinions entierement et exactement pareilles, non plus que deux visages. Leur plus propre qualité, c'est la diversité et discordance."* ["And perhaps there were never in the world two opinions entirely and exactly alike, any more than two faces. Their most intrinsic quality is diversity and discord."] (II: 37, 766, S598; cf. DB II, 364.)

Human diversity does not dismay Montaigne, but it is still what strikes him most. He still reacts as one man alone; he still presents his portrait as simply that of an individual. One element of his final thought is yet to come.

⋌ VI ⋊

THE SUBJECT AS MAN:
BOOK III

When Montaigne published Books I and II of the *Essais* in 1580, Book III lay eight years ahead and was probably not yet thought of. Foremost in his mind was his Italian trip, which was to last through most of 1581 and be followed immediately by two terms as mayor of Bordeaux. Then, after a year at home with his *Essais*, he was interrupted in the summer of 1586 by the siege of nearby Castillon and the plague that followed. Around April, 1587, he returned home and continued to write until about January, 1588, when he went to confer with Matignon about his forthcoming trip to Paris.

The earliest *Essais* had been well received. The king and the papal censor had been gracious; critics and anthologists like La Croix du Maine and Du Verdier had praised them highly; several authors had paid the tribute of borrowing; the great Belgian scholar Justus Lipsius had dubbed their author "the French Thales." As we have seen in Chapter I, the first edition had soon been followed by a second, a now vanished third, and a fourth, published in Paris; the three books of the fifth edition were to be published again in Paris, by one of the finest houses in France. The favor of the public, Montaigne writes, makes him a little bolder now than he had expected (III: 9, 942, S736).

The success of the *Essais* contributed not only to Montaigne's confidence but also to his sense of human unity and solidarity. So did his friendly contacts on his trip with people of other nations, tongues, and ways; the satisfaction of being singled out, not once but twice, to watch over the affairs of his city; the closeness and respect he came to feel for the people of Bordeaux (III: 10, 998–99, S781); and his admiration for the simple heroism of his rustic neighbors in the face of illness and death (III: 12, 1025–26, S802–3).

42

Already in the second chapter of Book III ("Of Repentance") Montaigne shows his new sense of unity. It is that of mankind that he proclaims first: *"Je propose une vie basse et sans lustre, c'est tout un. On attache aussi bien toute la philosophie morale à une vie populaire et privée que à une vie de plus riche estoffe; chaque homme porte la forme entiere de l'humaine condition."* ["I set forth a humble and inglorious life; that does not matter. You can tie up all moral philosophy with a common and private life just as well as with a life of richer stuff. Each man bears the entire form of man's estate."] (III: 2, 782, S611.) A few pages later he shows his new awareness of a bedrock unity and stability in every individual: *"Regardez un peu comment s'en porte nostre experience: il n'est personne, s'il s'escoute, qui ne descouvre en soy une forme sienne, une forme maistresse, qui luicte contre l'institution, et contre la tempeste des passions qui luy sont contraires."* ["Just consider the evidence of this in our own experience. There is no one who, if he listens to himself, does not discover in himself a pattern all his own, a ruling pattern, which struggles against education and against the tempest of the passions that oppose it."] (III: 2, 789, S615.)

The effect of these new convictions is enormous. If there is nothing but diversity in the individual and the race, what can anyone have to say to anyone else, or for that matter to himself? Montaigne is ready now to speak with more assurance, and for others as well as for Michel. His portrait is no longer of himself alone, but also of man.

Now, surer of his plan, he writes faster; surer of his reader, he demands more of his attention. Everything holds together, and he has much to say; he needs room to show the movement as well as the content of his thought. So he makes his chapters longer: the thirteen of Book III contrast with the fifty-seven of Book I and the thirty-seven of Book II; only one is short, and three are longer than any except the "Apology."

The principal subjects of the new chapters are the problem of public morality and the claims of honor against expediency (1); the rarity of true repentance, its doubtful place in the examined life, and the many phenomena that wrongly pass for it (2); Montaigne's favorite companies, attractive men, attractive women, and books (3); the value of diversion as our best resource against pain and grief (4); the vast importance of sex, the need for frankness about it, its negative relation to marriage (5); the cruelty of Europeans in the New World (6); the disadvantages of greatness (7); the art of vigorous discussion and the qualities it requires (8); vanity, travel, Montaigne's book, and impractical codes of morality (9); Montaigne's mayoralty and the value of a certain detachment from one's office (10); credulity about miracles and witchcraft (11); the heroism of Montaigne's peasant neighbors and the moral perfection of Socrates' simple humanity (12); the problems of unity and diversity and of knowledge, the uses of experience, the physical regimen of Montaigne, and the joy and dignity of life when lived in accordance with the human condition (13).

The main fruit of Montaigne's increased confidence is greater candor in what he reveals about himself, his book and his plan, and how man should live.

In 1580 he had spoken of his respect for the public as an obstacle to full self-revelation ("Au lecteur," 9, S2). Now that obstacle has shrunk: *"Je dy vray, non pas tout mon saoul, mais autant que je l'ose dire; et l'ose un peu plus en vieillissant . . ."* ["I speak the truth, not my fill of it, but as much as I dare speak; and I dare to do so a little more as I grow old . . ."] (III: 2, 783, S611.) He wants to be known just as he is, and dislikes even thoughts that are unpublishable (III: 5, 822, S642). He is more outspoken in his remarks about sex in general and his own sex life in "Sur des vers de Virgile" ["On Some Verses of Virgil"] (III: 5) and in his account, extending to copulation and defecation, of his physical regimen in "De l'experience" ["Of Experience"] (III: 13).

He studies himself more than any other subject; as he says, that is his metaphysics and his physics; for that is how we really learn to control our conduct.

J'aymerois mieux m'entendre bien en moy qu'en Ciceron. De l'experience que j'ay de moy, je trouve assez dequoy me faire sage, si j'estoy bon escholier. Qui remet en sa memoire l'excez de sa cholere passée, et jusques où cette fiévre l'emporta, voit la laideur de cette passion mieux que dans Aristote, et en conçoit une haine plus juste. . . . Escoutons y seulement; nous nous disons tout ce de quoy nous avons principalement besoing. (III: 13, 1051, S822.)

[I would rather be an authority on myself than on Cicero. In the experience I have of myself I find enough to make me wise, if I were a good scholar. He who calls back to mind the excess of his past anger, and how far this fever carried him away, sees the ugliness of this passion better than in Aristotle, and conceives a more justified hatred for it. . . . Let us only listen; we tell ourselves all we most need.]

Self-study is a school not only of morality but of human nature. By his long habit of mirroring his life in that of others, Montaigne has come to know others well. Often he understands his friends better than they do themselves and reveals to them their unrecognized motives. Though his subject is still himself, it now is also mankind.

In what he now calls a record of "the essays of my life" (III: 13, 1056, S826), his sense of his procedure is clearer. He writes his book for few men and few years (III: 9, 960, S751) in a backward region where he has no help, so that his book, though perhaps weaker, is more his own (III: 5, 853, S666–67). He adds but does not correct, for an author has no right to suppress what he has once mortgaged to the public (III: 9, 941, S736). He loves the free, gamboling poetic gait, and allows himself to wander; his ideas follow one another, but sometimes from a distance. His chapter titles are often more allusive than descriptive; he has no patience with artificial signposts or an inattentive reader (III: 9, 973–74, S761–62).

He finds his own work the hardest to judge, and places it now high, now low (III: 9, 918, S718). Though he knows his subject well, the main thing he has learned is how much he still has to learn (III: 13, 1052, S823). *"Je n'ay veu monstre et miracle au monde plus exprès que moy-mesme. . . . Plus je me hante et me connois, plus ma difformité m'estonne, moins je m'entens en moy."* ["I have seen no more evident monstrosity and miracle in the world than myself. . . . The more I frequent myself and know myself, the more my deformity astonishes me, and the less I understand myself."] (III: 11, 1006, S787.) Still he claims that he has thoroughly exposed his subject and leaves nothing about himself to be desired or guessed (III: 9, 961, S751).

Whatever he does, Montaigne is always ultimately a moralist; even self-study and the self-portrait have a moral as well as an intellectual purpose. He is dogmatic about the importance of conduct: *"La principale charge que nous ayons,"* he writes, *"c'est à chacun sa conduite"* ["The main responsibility of each of us is his own conduct"]; and after 1588 he adds: *"et est ce pour quoy nous sommes icy"* ["and that is what we are here for"] (III: 10, 984, S769–70).

One of the greatest moral questions is the balance of our duty to others and to ourselves. We tend to deny the latter in theory but to overcompensate for this in practice. The true point of our proper friendship to ourselves—salutary and regulated, not overindulgent —is to Montaigne a mystery of the temple of Pallas. The man who knows this point and practices both duties has attained the summit of human wisdom and of happiness (III: 10, 983–84, S769).

Often confused with this question is that of public and private life. Montaigne had protested from the first that private life is not *ipso facto* selfish nor public life unselfish (I: 39, 232, S174–75). He recognizes that our most honorable occupation is to serve the public and be useful to many. When he says he stays out of it partly from conscience, partly from laziness (III: 9, 929–30, S727), "laziness" seems to mean his willingness to let others rule and his distaste for mastery, whether active or passive (III: 7, 896, S700); and "conscience" his refusal to sacrifice this part of him. Public life demands a compromise morality; anyone who leaves it with clean breeches does so by a miracle. Hence Montaigne's little experience of it has left him rather disgusted (III: 9, 970, S758–59; cf. III: 1, *passim*).

Private life, though less glamorous, is more demanding. All we need in public is our mask, our "art," a semblance of virtue; in private we need our face, our nature, virtue itself.

> *Gaigner une bresche, conduire une ambassade, regir un peuple, ce sont actions esclatantes. Tancer, rire, vendre, payer, aymer, hayr et converser avec les siens et avec soymesme doucement et justement, ne relâcher point, ne se desmentir poinct, c'est chose plus rare, plus difficile et moins remerquable. Les vies retirées soustiennent par là, quoy qu'on die, des devoirs autant ou plus aspres que ne font les autres vies. (III: 2, 787, S614.)*

[To win through a breach, to conduct an embassy, to govern a people, these are dazzling actions. To scold, to laugh, to sell, to pay, to love, to hate, and to deal pleasantly and justly with our household and ourselves, not to let ourselves go, not to be false to ourselves, that is a rarer matter, more difficult and less noticeable. Therefore retired lives, whatever people may say, accomplish duties as harsh and strenuous as other lives, or more so.]

A private person, Montaigne maintains, is in quest of man's most legitimate knowledge: how to lead his life in conformity with its natural condition; more than others he needs an established inner pattern by which to test and judge his actions. Thus private life implies self-examination and self-control and leads to moral independence:

> J'ay mes loix et ma court pour juger de moy, et m'y adresse plus qu'ailleurs. . . . Il n'y a que vous qui sçache si vous estes lâche et cruel, ou loyal et devotieux; les autres ne vous voyent poinct; ils vous devinent par conjectures incertaines; ils voyent non tant vostre nature que vostre art. Par ainsi ne vous tenez pas à leur sentence; tenez vous à la vostre. (III: 2, 785, S613.)

> [I have my own laws and court to judge me, and I address myself to them more than anywhere else. . . . There is no one but yourself who knows whether you are cowardly and cruel, or loyal and devout. Others do not see you, they guess at you by uncertain conjectures; they see not so much your nature as your art. Therefore do not cling to their judgment; cling to your own.]

Montaigne's preference for private life no longer means withdrawal, but a balance that he often expresses as lending oneself to others but not giving oneself away. To him, proper self-possession is not only fair and equitable but essential for moral independence and wisdom.

Man would be happier and better, Montaigne finds, if he would accept himself for what he is. His failure to do so leads to unjustified self-disdain, which Montaigne combats with gentle mockery: *"Hé! pauvre homme, tu as assez d'incommoditez naturelles, sans les augmenter par ton invention; et es assez miserable de condition, sans l'estre par art."* ["Alas, poor man! You have enough natural ills without increasing them by your invention, and you are miserable enough by nature without being so by art."] [1] A more dangerous consequence is the temptation to try to be more than human: *"Ils veulent se mettre hors d'eux et eschapper à l'homme. C'est folie; au lieu de se transformer en anges, ils se transforment en bestes; au lieu de se hausser, ils s'abattent."* ["They want to get out of themselves and escape from the man. That is madness: instead of changing into angels, they change into beasts; instead of raising themselves, they lower themselves."] (III: 13, 1096, S856.) Another danger is to adopt lofty theories to cover our wretched practice (III: 9, 967–69, S756–58) and thus pile hypocrisy on top of moral shabbiness. For his part Montaigne accepts himself as he is, rarely repents, and questions the validity of most repentance unless it comes from God: *"Mes actions sont reglées et conformes à ce que je suis et à ma condition. Je ne puis faire mieux."* ["My actions are in order and conformity with what I am and with my condition. I can do no better."] (III: 2, 791, S617.)

Montaigne finds none of this impractical self-rejection in Christianity. As we shall see more fully later in Chapter VIII, he sees man's proper relation to God as a combination of complete submission with great freedom. In his view God has given us nature as a sure guide to our earthly salvation, and would have made us perfect had he expected us to be so.

A major and growing concern of Montaigne's in Book III is wholeness. For him age, which most of those who think about it— the aging and the aged—hail as a growth in wisdom and virtue, is really a diminution, a partial dying. As his decaying body seeks to dominate, Montaigne must defend himself against temperance as he once did against sensuality; for wisdom needs as much moderation as folly, and only thus can he be master of himself in every direction (III: 5, 818, S638–39). He despises the accidental repentance brought on by age, with its sluggish and rheumatic virtue. Old age, he finds, puts more wrinkles in our minds than on our faces; it is rare to find an aging soul that is not turning sour and musty: *"L'homme marche entier vers son croist et vers son décroist."* ["Man grows and dwindles in his entirety."] (III: 2, 793, 795, S619–20.)

The remedy is to struggle for balance. To keep his mind free and whole, he urges it to rescue itself from the aging process: *"Qu'il verdisse, qu'il fleurisse ce pendant, s'il peut, comme le guy sur un arbre mort."* ["Let it grow green, let it flourish meanwhile, if it can, like mistletoe on a dead tree."] (III: 5, 821, S641.) We must not let the years undermine our judgment, but still see with the

eyes of youth as well as those of age (III: 2, 793-94, S619). Only
thus can we be not merely young or merely old, but whole.

Another important aspect of wholeness for Montaigne is ver-
satility, by which he usually means the ability to live well and
happily on levels other than the most exalted. We must cultivate
this by habit. The fairest souls are the most adaptable: *"Je louerois
un' ame à divers estages, qui sçache et se tendre et se desmonter."*
["I would admire a soul with different levels, which can both be
tense and relax."] (III: 3, 796, 799, S621, 623.) In the final pages of
the *Essais* this is one of the key themes. Caesar and Alexander,
Brutus, both Catos, Epaminondas, and Scipio the Younger enjoyed
natural, simple pleasures in their free moments. Socrates, as usual,
is the best model. A brave soldier, a deep thinker given to medita-
tive trances, he was equally at home drinking the rest of the army
under the table or playing games with children. *"On a dequoy, et
ne doibt on jamais se lasser de presenter l'image de ce personnage
à tous patrons et formes de perfection."* ["We have material enough,
and we should never tire of presenting the picture of this man as
a pattern and ideal of all sorts of perfection."] (III: 13, 1090, S852.)

Montaigne is so concerned with self-acceptance that he often
seems to neglect self-improvement. His remarks have led many to
find him lax. He likes to talk about the soft and healthy pillow—
for a well-made head—of ignorance and incuriosity (III: 13, 1050–
51, S822), and to praise nature as a gentle guide whom we cannot
go wrong to follow (III: 13, 1094, S855). He finds both Catos severe
and troublesome, and is wary of their inimitable straining after
virtue (III: 13, 1089, S851). He mistrusts inner turmoil and claims
not to know how to foster quarrels and conflict within himself
(II: 11, 406, S311). Unlike Socrates, he says, he has not used reason
to correct his natural disposition: *"Je me laisse aller, comme je suis
venu, je ne combats rien."* ["I let myself go as I have come. I combat
nothing."] (III: 12, 1037, S811.)

However, as we have noted, he believes that the individual must
be his own judge, and he does not take this duty lightly; his aim
is not self-indulgence but self-mastery. If his powers of resistance
are slight and his quota of virtue an accidental innocence, still he
controls his vices and keeps them from infecting his judgment and
supporting one another: *"Les miens, je les ay retranchez et contrains*

le plus seuls et les plus simples que j'ay peu." ["Mine I have cut down and constrained to be as solitary and simple as I could."] (II: 11, 407–8, S312.) The self-mastery he wants must strive to be complete: "*Esclave, je ne le doibts estre que de la raison, encore ne puis-je bien en venir à bout.*" ["A slave I must be only to reason, and even that I can scarcely manage."] (III: 1, 772, S603.)

The honesty needed for true self-revelation, for daring to say all that he dares to do (III: 5, 822, S642), has been a moral discipline that more men should practice. Self-portrayal is a school of consistency, for it commits a man to be what he says he is and practice what he preaches (III: 9, 958, 969, S749, 758). Even more important is habit, by which we can give our life the form we choose (III: 13, 1058, 1061, S827, 830); which has made Montaigne what he is, changing his form into substance, and fortune into nature; and which now, after Aristotle, he calls a second nature, no less powerful than the first (III: 10, 987, S772). His sense of how habit shapes us explains his at first puzzling statement about the Stoics: "*Ce que ceux-là faisoient par vertu, je me duits à le faire par complexion.*" ["What those men did by virtue, I train myself to do by disposition."] (III: 10, 997, S780.) His *complexion* is a second nature formed by habit. Once again self-acceptance is not the opposite of self-control but the means to it.

More than ever, Montaigne's ideal is not so much nature as a kind of perfected human nature. Even in the chapter most concerned with setting nature above art, "De la phisionomie" ["Of Physiognomy"] (III: 12), where he rejects premeditation of death in favor of trust in nature and urges us to hold a school of stupidity if necessary, his examples of natural men, his peasant neighbors, are less heroes than correctives. His real hero is Socrates, who can teach us—as the peasants cannot—to find in us such little learning as we need to live happily and well. On the simplest, most vulgar and natural motives and ideas of men he constructed the strongest and loftiest actions and morals ever. He accepted our condition and followed nature, but also improved his nature by reason and habit. Whereas the peasants are good, he is perfect; whereas they are models, he is not only model but guide. Their virtue is natural; his is both natural and fully human.

As I hope to have shown, Montaigne is more like Socrates than he is willing to claim. By the time he publishes Book III of the *Essais,* he has done much to combat vice by reason and to fashion himself along good lines. But as a self-portrayer, he cannot very well say so without alienating his reader—as many "confessors" have proven since his day. He has too much taste, humor—yes, and modesty—to make himself his hero. Ten years before, in the "Apology," Pyrrho had served as a surrogate. Now his man is Socrates.[2]

More and more, Montaigne's favorite term of praise comes to be no longer "natural" but "human." The best opinions, he finds, are the most solid, which is to say *"les plus humaines et nostres"* ["most human and most our own"] (III: 13, 1094, S855). Epaminondas is one of the best men ever because even in violence he maintained his goodness and humanity (III: 1, 780, S609); Vulcan's kindness to his unfaithful wife Venus is of *"une humanité à la verité plus qu'humaine"* ["a humanity truly more than human"] (III: 5, 842, S658). The notion is central in his final formulations of human wisdom: to live appropriately, to enjoy our being rightfully, and especially this: *"Il n'est rien si beau et legitime que de bien faire l'homme et deuëment."* ["There is nothing so beautiful and legitimate as to play the man well and properly."] [3]

In the essays of 1578–80, when Montaigne's illness had dispelled any remnants of his early wariness of life, we noted a new stress on man's resources, especially for wisdom and happiness. In Book III this becomes a major theme.

Now that pain is an integral part of Montaigne's life he learns to accept it serenely and—like Socrates early in the *Phaedo*—to stress its interdependence with pleasure. Much of the art of living lies in learning to harmonize the two.

> *Il faut apprendre à souffrir ce qu'on ne peut eviter. Nostre vie est composée, comme l'armonie du monde, de choses contraires, aussi de divers tons, douz et aspres, aigus et plats, mols et graves. Le musicien qui n'en aymeroit que les uns, que voudroit il dire? Il faut qu'il s'en sçache servir en commun et les mesler. Et nous aussi, les biens et les maux, qui sont consubstantiels à nostre vie. Nostre estre ne peut sans ce meslange, et y est l'une bande non moins necessaire que l'autre.* (III: 13, 1068, S835.)
>
> [We must learn to endure what we cannot avoid. Our life is composed, like the harmony of the world, of contrary things, also of different tones, sweet and harsh, sharp and flat, soft and loud. If a

musician liked only one kind, what would he have to say? He must
know how to use them together and blend them. And so we must
do with good and evil, which are consubstantial with our life. Our
existence is impossible without this mixture, and one element is no
less necessary for it than the other.]

The final pages of the *Essais* are a hymn of gratitude for the
legitimate joys of life. Too many men are content to pass the time,
as though life were something to get over with. Montaigne knows
that it is worth prizing even in its decline, and that we are to blame
if we let it pass by unenjoyed. The key to happy living is the attention and skill of the artist in life: *"Il y a du mesnage à la jouyr; je
la jouys au double des autres, car la mesure en la jouyssance depend
du plus ou moins d'application que nous y prestons."* ["It takes management to enjoy it. I enjoy it twice as much as others, for the
measure of enjoyment depends on the greater or lesser application
that we lend it."] (III: 13, 1092, S853.)

Most men pass over proper pleasures for empty hopes and fancies, and seek other conditions because they fail to understand and
accept their own. Not so Montaigne:

> *Pour moy donc, j'ayme la vie et la cultive telle qu'il a pleu à
> Dieu nous l'octroier. . . . J'accepte de bon cœur . . . ce que nature
> a faict pour moy, et m'en agrée et l'en remercie. On fait tort à ce
> grand et tout puissant donneur de refuser son don, l'alterer et
> desfigurer.*[4]

> [As for me, then, I love life and cultivate it just as God has been
> pleased to grant it to us. . . . I accept with all my heart . . . what
> nature has done for me, and I am pleased with myself that I do and
> thank her for it. We wrong that great and all-powerful Giver by
> refusing his gift, altering it, and disfiguring it.]

Sometime in his last four years of life Montaigne summed it up
by adding: *"Tout bon il a faict tout bon."* ["Himself all good, he
has made all things good."]

✥ VII ✥

THE FINAL ADDITIONS

Montaigne wrote no more books or chapters after 1588; but in his four remaining years of life he went on working on his *Essais,* adding about a thousand passages—about a quarter of the entire book—partly on separate pieces of paper but mainly on the margins of an unbound copy of his 1588 edition, the Bordeaux Copy, mentioned in Chapter I. This is the basic text of the final *Essais.* On the frontispiece he placed a confident new epigraph, *"Viresque acquirit eundo."* ["He acquires strength as he goes."]

These manuscript additions reveal a much more careful writer than Montaigne claims to be. Often several successive versions show him struggling to find the best formulation of an idea; once in a while, dissatisfied, he crosses a whole passage out. His normal aims are strength and clarity of expression.

This final material shows no marked changes in thought or attitude from that of 1588, but a further sharpening of Montaigne's views: greater readiness to contradict what he had written earlier, greater boldness manifested mainly in five areas: self-revelation, obscenity, his book and his plan, the evils of the religion of his day, and his independent morality.

Montaigne had presented himself rather disparagingly from the first; now he becomes more specific about such real defects as an avaricious stage when he lied about his money (I: 14, 65, S44), or the idleness, coolness, and self-centeredness for which he is reproached (I: 26, 175, S130). Often he portrays himself in a comic light, as when he discusses his decrepit old age (III: 10, 987–88, S772–73) and the supposed maturation of aging, which is really *"un mouvement d'yvroigne titubant, vertigineux, informe"* ["a drunkard's motion, staggering, dizzy, wobbling"] (III: 9, 942, S736). To illustrate the statement that no quality embraces us purely and universally, he sketches himself calling his valet a clown or a calf—but later a fine fellow—and himself a confounded fool—but not intending that to be his definition (I: 38, 230, S173).

Montaigne is freer now in using obscenity to remind us of our "peacock's feet" (III: 5, 855, S669). He illustrates our lack of self-control by the unruly liberty of the male member—and then defends it comically against our equally seditious other parts (I: 21, 100–1, S72–73). His treatment of sex in "Sur des vers de Virgile" ["On Some Verses of Virgil"] (III:5) grows more concrete and outspoken. Of his penis he now writes: *"Chacune de mes pieces me faict esgalement moy que toute autre. Et nulle autre ne me faict plus proprement homme que cette-cy."* ["Each one of my parts makes me myself just as much as every other one. And no other makes me more properly a man than this one."] (III: 5, 866, S677.) He imagines philosophers of a certain type trying to square the circle while perched on their wives (III: 13, 1087, S850), and ends his next-to-last paragraph with the reminder: *"Et au plus eslevé throne du monde, si ne sommes assis que sus nostre cul."* ["And on the loftiest throne in the world we are still sitting only on our own rump."] (III: 13, 1096, S857.) Other examples are equally vivid. The aim of it all is not only comic but didactic: an exemplary declaration of the whole truth.

> *Je dois au publiq universellement mon pourtrait. . . . Qui desniaise-roit l'homme d'une si scrupuleuse superstition verbale n'apporteroit pas grande perte au monde. Nostre vie est partie en folie, partie en prudence. Qui n'en escrit que reveremment et regulierement, il en laisse en arriere plus de la moitié.* (III: 5, 866–67, S677–78.)
>
> [I owe a complete portrait of myself to the public. . . . Whoever would wean man of the folly of such a scrupulous verbal superstition would do the world no great harm. Our life is part folly, part wisdom. Whoever writes about it only reverently and according to the rules leaves out more than half of it.]

Montaigne continues to reveal new insights into his book and his plan. He now dares to speak solely of himself, but he knows he can view himself with detachment as he would a neighbor or a tree (III: 8, 921, S720). His broader subject is more and more man in general (II: 10, 396, S303) and man in all his potentiality: not only what has actually happened, but whatever can happen (I: 21, 104,

S75). He is proud of the richness of his material and wants to be known for that, not for his language (I: 40, 245, S184–85) or his order (II: 27, 678, S528–29). No man, he feels sure, has ever treated a subject he knew better, penetrated his material more deeply, or plucked its limbs and consequences cleaner (III: 2, 783, S611). His book may know many things that he no longer knows; and if he is wiser than it, it may be richer than he (II: 8, 383, S293). It is always one and the same; his additions are extra ornaments that do not really change it (III: 9, 941, S736).

Substantial additions to two chapters of Book II show dramatically, by their contrast with the original version, Montaigne's deepened sense of his plan. We have seen how he had concluded "Of Practice" (II: 6) around 1574 by saying, after Pliny, that self-scrutiny can make a man a good education to himself, and that his book is a lesson not for others but for himself. Now he adds three pages about his plan. It is a thorny but invaluable enterprise, he finds, to plumb the opaque depths of the mind, follow its wanderings, and hold it still to paint its portrait. Only superficial self-study is presumptuous; the serious kind is humbling. Candor should be the rule; if he thought himself really good and wise, he would shout it from the housetops. His portrait is a cadaver in which he exposes himself— that is to say his thoughts—entire: what he writes is not his deeds, but himself, his essence. Self-portrayal is a sort of self-formation: *"Encore se faut-il testoner, encore se faut-il ordonner et renger pour sortir en place. Or je me pare sans cesse, car je me descris sans cesse."* ["Even so one must spruce up, even so one must present oneself in an orderly arrangement, if one would go out in public. Now, I am constantly adorning myself, for I am constantly describing myself."] (II: 6, 357–60, S272–75.)

In the original version of "Giving the Lie" (II: 18) Montaigne had been very deprecating: his portrait was intended not for a public square but for a library nook, to amuse a relative or a friend. Now he speaks of it as a useful and enjoyable project, a diversion from annoying thoughts, a source of purpose, discipline, and insight. His commitment is complete; he makes this his study, his work, and his trade, and binds himself to keep an enduring account, with all his faith and all his strength. One result has been to fashion himself:

Moulant sur moy cette figure, il m'a fallu si souvent dresser et composer pour m'extraire, que le patron s'en est fermy et aucunement formé soy-mesmes. Me peignant pour autruy, je me suis peint en moy de couleurs plus nettes que n'estoyent les miennes premieres. Je n'ay pas plus faict mon livre que mon livre m'a faict, livre consubstantiel à son autheur, d'une occupation propre, membre de ma vie. (II: 18, 647–49, S504–5.)
[In modeling this figure upon myself, I have had to fashion and compose myself so often to bring myself out, that the model itself has to some extent grown firm and taken shape. Painting myself for others, I have painted my inward self with colors clearer than my original ones. I have no more made my book than my book has made me—a book consubstantial with its author, concerned with my own self, an integral part of my life.]

Montaigne's religious position, combining freedom of thought with submissiveness, seems a little freer now. He never made any of the changes suggested by the papal censors, but now he adds two notes in his own defense and enlarges one statement of his submission to the Church.[1]

His indignation is now outspoken against the fomenters of religious civil war, especially the Protestants, whom he represents as overthrowing law and order, dismembering their mother and tossing the pieces to her enemies, teaching brother to hate brother, calling on the devils and furies for aid—in short, heading straight for damnation—and this under color of seeking salvation and supporting the divine word (III: 12, 1020, S798). However, their opponents are little better; both sides use religion with such horrible impudence that it is hard to believe they are doctrinally opposed. Under Henry III the Protestants claimed, and the Catholics denied, the subject's right to revolt against the king in the name of conscience; under Henry IV both sides did an about-face. Both sides twist the religion of love and mercy into a pretext for every kind of wickedness. We use our piety and zeal only to inflame our hatred, cruelty, ambition, avarice, detraction, rebellion. Made to extirpate vices, Christianity as we practice it covers them, fosters them, incites them (II: 12, 420–21, S323–24).

Montaigne's final moral pronouncements often dwell on independence, virtue as pleasure, integrity, and humanness. More than ever he insists on our proper concern with ourselves (III: 9, 929, S726) and on a moral autonomy that includes firm self-government

(I: 39, 237, S178). Each man must find his own form of this: *"Puis que la philosophie n'a sçeu trouver aucune voye pour la tranquillité qui fust bonne en commun, que chacun la cherche en son particulier."* ["Since philosophy has not been able to find a way to tranquillity that is suitable to all, let everyone seek it individually."] (II: 16, 605–6, S471.)

More and more, he praises pleasure—though insisting on moderation in its pursuit—and likes to remind us that it is the object of virtue. Actually the relation is closer yet. Voluptuousness of the baser sort offers weak enjoyment, great hardships, a kind of penance in the satiety that follows. But virtue is itself our highest pleasure, and even its pursuit is joyous (I: 20, 80–81, S56–57).

> *La vertu . . . est . . . logée dans une belle plaine fertile et fleurissante, d'où elle voit bien souz soy toutes choses; mais si peut on y arriver, qui en sçait l'adresse, par des routes ombrageuses, gazonnées et doux fleurantes, plaisamment et d'une pante facile et polie, comme est celle des voutes celestes. . . .*
>
> *. . . C'est la mere nourrice des plaisirs humains. En les rendant justes, elle les rend seurs et purs. . . . Elle aime la vie, elle aime la beauté et la gloire et la santé. Mais son office propre et particulier, c'est sçavoir user de ces biens là regléement, et les sçavoir perdre constamment . . .* (I: 26, 160–62, S119–20.)
>
> [Virtue . . . is . . . established in a beautiful plain, fertile and flowering, from where, to be sure, she sees all things beneath her; but you can get there, if you know the way, by shady, grassy, sweetly flowering roads, pleasantly, by an easy smooth slope, like that of the celestial vaults. . . .
>
> . . . She is the nursing mother of human pleasures. By making them just, she makes them sure and pure. . . . She loves life, she loves beauty and glory and health. But her own particular task is to know how to enjoy those blessings with temperance, and to lose them with fortitude . . .]

Integrity is a major and ever-growing concern of Montaigne's. One of its aspects is truth, which he says we must love for itself as the first and fundamental part of virtue. Our word must always be sacred; even a promise extracted by fear must be kept (III: 1, 779, S608). Happily, Montaigne's own soul naturally shuns lying and hates even to think a lie (II: 17, 631, S491).

Integrity requires a kind of consistency which Montaigne sets very high. Whereas twenty years before he had earnestly aspired to a noble death, now he wants one that will not belie his life (I: 7,

33, S20): *"Je ne me suis pas attendu d'attacher monstrueusement la queuë d'un philosophe à la teste et au corps d'un homme perdu . . ."* ["I have made no effort to attach, monstrously, the tail of a philosopher to the head and body of a dissipated man . . ."] [2]

"Follow nature" is still a favorite refrain for Montaigne. We need not worry about the workings of the universe, he finds, for we know that God is its creator and nature his benign agent. She has given us not only feet to walk with, but also wisdom to guide our steps. *"Le plus simplement se commettre à nature, c'est s'y commettre le plus sagement."* ["The more simply we trust to Nature, the more wisely we trust to her."] (III: 13, 1050, S822.)

To follow nature in this way is to become truly human. Montaigne now finds man innately capable not only of happiness and wisdom but also of a virtue which is all our own and the only kind he really likes. In his boldest plea for moral autonomy, he now criticizes all other virtue, even that motivated by law and religion, as a kind of slave morality.

> *Diray-je cecy en passant: que je voy tenir en plus de prix qu'elle ne vaut, qui est seule quasi en usage entre nous, certaine image de preud'homie scholastique, serve des preceptes, contraincte soubs l'esperance et la crainte? Je l'aime telle que les loix et religions non facent, mais parfacent et authorisent, qui se sente de quoy se soustenir sans aide, née en nous de ses propres racines par la semence de la raison universelle empreinte en tout homme non desnaturé. Cette raison, qui redresse Socrates de son vicieux ply, le rend obeïssant aux hommes et aux Dieux qui commandent en sa ville, courageux en la mort, non parce que son ame est immortelle, mais par ce qu'il est mortel.* (III: 12, 1037, S811.)

> [Shall I say this in passing: that I see held in greater price than it is worth a certain idea of scholastic probity, almost the only one practiced among us, a slave to precepts, held down beneath fear and hope? What I like is the virtue that laws and religions do not make but perfect and authorize, that feels in itself enough to sustain itself without help, born in us from its own roots, from the seed of universal reason that is implanted in every man who is not denatured. This reason, which straightens Socrates from his inclination to vice, makes him obedient to the men and gods who command in his city, courageous in death not because his soul is immortal but because he is mortal.]

Montaigne's pride in humanness is what gives him a conscience content with itself, not as the conscience of an angel or a horse, but as the conscience of a man (III: 2, 784, S612). His faith is in the broad highroad of humanity. The ecstasies and daemon even of a Socrates alarm him; the fairest lives, he finds, avoid miracles and eccentricity and conform to the common human pattern. The great thing in life is living—simply, gratefully, as human beings.

Nous sommes de grands fols: "Il a passé sa vie en oisiveté, disons nous; je n'ay rien faict d'aujourd' huy.—Quoy, avez vous pas vescu? C'est non seulement la fondamentale, mais la plus illustre de vos occupations.—Si on m'eust mis au propre des grands maniements, j'eusse montré ce que je sçavois faire.—Avez vous sceu mediter et manier vostre vie? vous avez faict la plus grande besoigne de toutes." . . . *Composer nos meurs est nostre office, non pas composer des livres, et gaigner, non pas des batailles et provinces, mais l'ordre et tranquillité à nostre conduite. Nostre grand et glorieux chef-d'œuvre, c'est vivre à propos.* (III: 13, 1088, S850–51; cf. 1096, S856–57.)

[We are great fools. "He has spent his life in idleness," we say; "I have done nothing today." What, have you not lived? That is not only the fundamental but the most illustrious of your occupations. "If I had been placed in a position to manage great affairs, I would have shown what I could do." Have you been able to think out and manage your life? You have done the greatest task of all. . . . To compose our characters is our duty, not to compose books, and to win, not battles and provinces, but order and tranquillity in our conduct. Our great and glorious masterpiece is to live appropriately.]

Montaigne's determination to express himself clearly and fully makes him readier now to modify, or even contradict, some of his earlier views. Without disavowing the extreme withdrawal expressed by his early remark that the greatest thing in the world is to know how to belong to oneself (I: 39, 236, S178), he seems to modify it now by this addition: *"Qui ne vit aucunement à autruy, ne vit guère à soy."* ["He who lives not at all unto others, hardly lives unto himself."] (III: 10, 984, S769.) He shows his confirmed rejection of a certain Stoicism when he changes an introduction to Cato the Elder from *"la vraye image de la vertu Stoique"* ["the true image of Stoic virtue"] to *"Ce censeur et correcteur des autres"* ["That censor and corrector of others"] (II: 2, 324, S246; cf. DB I, 281).

A fruitful modification of an earlier position is in Montaigne's view of the arbitrariness of the human soul, its freedom to make what it will of the data furnished it by the senses. In one of his earliest chapters (I: 14) he had wondered just how far this freedom went and decided it could help against poverty and death but hardly against pain, which we can merely resist. His main early use of the theme is in the "Apology for Raymond Sebond" (II: 12), as a proof of our ignorance. The infinite diversity of human opinion, he says, the fact that wine tastes different to a healthy man and to an invalid, proves that things lodge in us not in their own form and essence, but as we please (545, S422).

In Montaigne's final additions, every reference to the arbitrariness of the soul shows it to be an absolute guarantee of our capacity to be happy. The question he had raised in his early chapter title, whether the taste of good and evil depends in large part on our opinion of them, is now answered in that same chapter with a resounding affirmative.

> L'ame . . . renge à soy et à son estat, quel qu'il soit, les sentiments du corps et tous autres accidens. . . . Il n'y a raison, ny prescription, ny force, qui puisse contre son inclination et son chois. De tant de milliers de biais qu'elle a en sa disposition, donnons-luy en un propre à nostre repos et conservation, nous voilà non couvers seulemant de toute offence, mais gratifiez mesmes et flattez, si bon luy semble, des offences et des maux. (I: 14, 57, S39; cf. 67, S46.)

> [The soul . . . molds to itself and to its every condition the feelings of the body and all other accidents. . . . There is no reason, prescription, or might that has power against its inclination and its choice. Out of the many thousands of attitudes at its disposal, let us give it one conducive to our repose and preservation, and we shall be not only sheltered from all harm, but even gratified and flattered, if it please, by ills and pains.]

The happy paradox that this source of our ignorance is a guarantee of our happiness is even clearer elsewhere:

> Les choses, à part elles, ont peut estre leurs poids et mesures et conditions; mais au dedans, en nous, elle [l'ame] les leur taille comme elle l'entend....... La santé, la conscience, l'authorité, la science, la richesse, la beauté et leurs contraires se despouillent à l'entrée, et reçoivent de l'ame nouvelle vesture, et de la teinture qu'il lui plaist: brune, verte, claire, obscure, aigre, douce, profonde, superficielle, et qu'il plaist à chacune d'elles; car......chacune est Royne en son estat. Parquoy ne prenons plus excuse des externes qualitez des choses: c'est à nous à nous en rendre compte. Nostre bien et nostre mal ne tient qu'à nous. (I: 50, 290, S220.)

> [Things in themselves may have their own weights and measures and qualities; but once inside, within us, she [the soul] allots them their qualities as she sees fit. . . . Health, conscience, authority, knowledge,

riches, beauty, and their opposites—all are stripped on entry and receive from the soul new clothing, and the coloring that she chooses—brown, green, bright, dark, bitter, sweet, deep, superficial—and which each individual soul chooses; for . . . each one is queen in her realm. Wherefore let us no longer make the external qualities of things our excuse; it is up to us to reckon them as we will. Our good and our ill depend on ourselves alone.]

Montaigne's view of death, as we noted, undergoes a complete change. In one of his earliest chapters he had called it the goal of our career, the necessary object of our aim (I: 20, 82, S57). Before 1580 he had moved to the position that philosophy is what teaches us to live; by 1588 he had advised us to give up premeditation and trust ourselves to nature. Now he contradicts his early view and treats learning to die as a minor matter.

Si nous n'avons sçeu vivre, c'est injustice de nous apprendre à mourir, et de difformer la fin de son tout. Si nous avons sçeu vivre constamment et tranquillement, nous sçaurons mourir de mesme. . . . Il m'est advis que c'est bien le bout, non pourtant le but de la vie; c'est sa fin, son extremité, non pourtant son object. Elle doit estre elle mesme à soy sa visée, son dessein . . . Au nombre de plusieurs autres offices que comprend ce general et principal chapitre de sçavoir vivre, est cet article de sçavoir mourir; et des plus legers si nostre crainte ne luy donnoit poids. (III: 12, 1028–29, S805.)

[If we have not known how to live, it is wrong to teach us how to die, and make the end inconsistent with the whole. If we have known how to live steadfastly and tranquilly, we shall know how to die in the same way. . . . It seems to me that death is indeed the end, but not therefore the goal, of life; it is its finish, its extremity, but not therefore its object. Life should be an aim unto itself, a purpose unto itself . . . Among the many other duties comprised in this general and principal chapter on knowing how to live is this article on knowing how to die; and it is one of the lightest, if our fear did not give it weight.]

In these final years Montaigne contradicts his early view that pain is always to be avoided. By 1588 he had come to stress its interdependence with pleasure and to urge us to harmonize the two. Now he goes so far as to argue that to reject pain is to reject the human condition itself. Fifteen years earlier, before his illness, he had written in the "Apology": *"La misere de nostre condition porte que nous n'avons pas tant à jouir qu'à fuir . . . Le n'avoir point de mal, c'est le plus avoir de bien que l'homme puisse esperer . . ."*

["The wretchedness of our condition makes us have less to enjoy than to avoid . . . To have no ill is to have the most good that man can hope for."] Faithful to his principle of not correcting what he has once written, he leaves these statements unchanged; but now, as we noted briefly earlier, his sense of the goodness of life impels him to add this rebuttal:

> *Je suis content de n'estre pas malade; mais, si je le suis, je veux sçavoir que je le suis; et, si on me cauterise ou incise, je le veux sentir. De vray, qui desracineroit la cognoissance du mal, il extirperoit quand et quand la cognoissance de la volupté, et en fin aneantiroit l'homme . . . Le mal est à l'homme bien à son tour. Ny la douleur ne luy est tousjours à fuir, ny la volupté tousjours à suivre.* (II: 12, 472–73, S363–64.)
>
> [I am glad not to be sick; but if I am, I want to know I am; and if they cauterize or incise me, I want to feel it. In truth, he who would eradicate the knowledge of evil would at the same time extirpate the knowledge of pleasure, and in fine would annihilate man . . . Evil is in its turn a good to man. Neither is pain always something for him to flee, nor pleasure always for him to pursue.]

One curious addition that Montaigne made after 1588 appears to be a substitution and a corrective. In the original version of the "Apology for Raymond Sebond," speaking of *le vulgaire* (the vulgar, the common herd; not a social class, but the unthinking opposites of the sage) and the credulous temerity that leads them, once any part of their belief has been shaken, to abandon the rest, Montaigne writes about them: *"et tout le monde est quasi de ce genre"* ["and almost everyone is of this sort"].[3] Sometime after 1588 he crosses out this interpolation. During the same years he adds a similar remark in the one other passage in the "Apology" where he discusses the vulgar. We should not, he had written, accept all probabilities that we cannot disprove; for if we did, the belief of the vulgar and the common people would be as easy to turn as a weathercock. After 1588 he deletes "and the common people" and adds, after "the vulgar," *"et nous sommes tous du vulgaire"* ["and we all are of the vulgar"].

Now the passages are over a hundred pages apart, and the ink looks different. Several things suggest, however, that the second is in effect a substitution for the first. Both the context and much of the sense—the credulity and the universality of the vulgar—are the same. If Montaigne had merely changed the phrasing of the first passage, it would have implied that he had Protestant leanings and was on the road to atheism; which is obviously false. I suspect that as he reread the chapter, he found the first interpolation supercilious and cut it out; then later, reading on, he found a perfect context for his comment in its altered form.

Montaigne's early training and writing—his friendship with La Boétie, his inscription on retiring, his bookish and rather Stoical early chapters—had been those of a humanist. As a humanist, he had little use for the vulgar; he had learned from Horace and others that they were to be hated and thrust aside.

His attitude before 1580 is consistently scornful of them as base and vile. They are slaves to custom, gullible as children, a prey to silly delusions and mad imaginings, cowardly and cruel in victory, brutishly stupid in their refusal to think of death. In a single list of their attributes, already noted (Chapter III), contrasting them with the sage, who is farther from them than heaven from earth, he describes them as a mob, ignorant, stupid, asleep, base, servile, full of fever and fright, unstable, constantly driven to and fro by their passions, wholly dependent on others.[4]

After 1588 Montaigne deletes three of these amenities: "ignorant," "asleep," and "full of fever and fright." Already, from 1580 on, a marked difference is discernible in his treatment of the vulgar. Though he still often shows scorn, this is now balanced by praise. Once he recognizes their difference from his kind only to insist that we need to talk their language, for all affairs are conducted with "humble and vulgar" souls, and these are often as well regulated as the subtler ones (III: 3, 797–98, S622). In his next-to-last chapter, "Of Physiognomy," he praises their obedience to nature. Socrates, he says, constructed the finest life and morality that ever were from the commonest ideas and the most vulgar and natural motives (III: 12, 1014, S793). Every day human learning must turn for models of conduct to the traces of nature's teaching that we still observe in the lives of *"cette tourbe rustique d'hommes impolis"* ["that rustic mob of unpolished men"]. If, as we like to say, it is stupidity that makes them brave, we had better hold a school of it (III: 12, 1026, 1029, S803, 805).

There is paradox in all this, to be sure; and Montaigne's "mob" is now the peasants, whose trust in nature makes them the truest philosophers (II: 17, 644, S501). However, the main change is that now, more than ever before, he identifies himself proudly—and with little suggestion of paradox—with the common people. Twice he writes that he is of the common sort; he calls his life common and private, his soul low and common, his opinions and conduct low and humble.[5] He urges anyone who cannot attain the noble impassibility of the Stoics to take refuge in the bosom of *"cette mienne stupidité populaire"* ["this plebeian stupidity of mine"] (III: 10, 997, S780). More and more, the term *vulgaire* is virtually equated with *human*; and that, as we have seen, is Montaigne's highest praise.

The clearest illustration of Montaine's change of attitude is in his change of statement, just noted, from "almost everyone is" to "we all are" members of the vulgar. Now it is *we*, not *they;* now it is all mankind, and Montaigne is proud of mankind. His sense of human solidarity is now complete, and with it the humanization of the humanist.

·ᐧ VIII ᐧ·

RELIGION

Though we have already spoken in passing of Montaigne's religion (pp. 6–9, 13, 24, 27–28, 48, 56), it offers problems enough, and has been variously enough assessed, to deserve special treatment.

The first and most official reaction to it came in 1581 from the papal censor, the Master of the Sacred Palace. His criticisms were mild and generally minor: for using the word "fortune" too often, praising heretics as poets, excusing Julian the Apostate, demanding that a person be free from evil impulses when praying, condemning as cruelty anything that goes beyond plain death, and urging that a child be brought up able to do anything and doing good only by free choice—and "other things of that sort" which Montaigne does not bother to specify.[1] Only the last two are substantial, and on one of these, torture, it was the Church that was to come around to Montaigne's position. The censors said that they honored his intention and affection for the Church, and left it to him to cut out, on republication, anything he found too licentious, and the uses of the word "fortune." He never made the changes, but added two passages explaining his casual references to fortune and maintaining that heretics may be good poets, and enlarged one statement disavowing anything he may have said in ignorance or inadvertence against the prescriptions of the Catholic Church, "in which I die and in which I was born."[2] Another addition in the same chapter ("Of Prayers," I: 56) seems to exlain that his sticking to his guns is an exercise of the right of the layman to express his opinions, however ill-founded, on matters of theology:

> *Je propose les fantasies humaines et miennes, simplement comme humaines fantasies . . . ; matiere d'opinion, non matiere de foy; ce que je discours selon moy, non ce que je croy selon Dieu, comme les enfans*

65

*proposent leurs essais; instruisables, non instruisants; d'une maniere
laïque, non clericale, mais très-religieuse tousjours.* (I: 56, 308–9, S234.)

[I set forth notions that are human and my own, simply as human
notions . . . ; matter of opinion, not matter of faith; what I reason
out according to me, not what I believe according to God; as children
set forth their essays to be instructed, not to instruct; in a lay manner,
not clerical, but always very religious.]

Montaigne's contemporaries accepted his religion as sincere, and
for two generations his Pyrrhonistic fideism was widely used by
Counter-Reformers against Protestant faith in individual reason.
However, from the 1620's on Garasse, Mersenne, and others condemned the Christian Pyrrhonists as indifferent at best and free-
thinking atheists at worst. Descartes's strong case for reason left
Montaigne as the suspect friend of such learned freethinkers as
Gabriel Naudé and Guy Patin. More and more attacks came, especially on moral grounds, from various religious quarters: Pascal and
other Jansenists, Bossuet, Malebranche. In 1676 the *Essais* were
placed on the Index.[3]

For the following century Montaigne, condemned by the Church,
was generally adopted by its adversaries as an enemy of dogma, a
tolerant sage in an age of fanaticism, a *philosophe* before the fact.[4]
Most nineteenth-century readers, more historically minded, were
more doubtful about just where Montaigne stood, and many pro-
claimed his religious sincerity; but the most searching and eloquent
study of the question, Sainte-Beuve's *Port-Royal* (composed in 1837,
published in 1842) pronounced him areligious in most of his work
and at heart, in the central "Apology for Raymond Sebond," a perfidious enemy of Christianity.[5] Though in all his later writings on
Montaigne Sainte-Beuve never repeated this charge, it was widely
read and quoted. In the present century a leading Montaigne
scholar, Dr. Arthur Armaingaud, who had once been Sainte-Beuve's
secretary, expounded a similar view, as did André Gide.

Heightened insight into the religious question in Montaigne's
time and greater awareness of his life and role have led most Montaigne scholars today—many of them Catholic churchmen—to a
conviction of Montaigne's religious sincerity.[6] A recent pope, Pius
XII, on the occasion of the canonization of Montaigne's niece Saint
Jeanne de Lestonnac, credited him with having saved her for

Catholicism in her childhood and expressed his wish and belief that before long the *Essais* might be removed from the Index.[7] Though today opinions vary on important aspects of Montaigne's religion, there seems to be a consensus that his faith was sincere.

Certainly Montaigne's life was that of a thoughtful and tolerant but unwavering Catholic. Tolerance was nothing new in his family, since one sister, the elder Jeanne de Lestonnac, and one brother, Thomas de Beauregard, were Protestants. Even before their conversion the question must have been a live one in the religiously divided region where they lived; and it was as an antidote to Lutheranism and atheism that Pierre Bunel, no later than 1546, gave Sebond's book to Montaigne's father. Montaigne tells us that he himself was once neglectful of certain points of Catholic observance (I: 27, 181, S134–35) but learned later that these were as solidly based as any; that compassion for their misery sometimes almost reconciled him to the Protestants and would have tempted him as a youth if anything could.[8] However, every glimpse we have of him, from the 1560's on, clearly shows his stanch Catholicism. His friend La Boétie favored correction of certain Catholic abuses but then firm treatment of the Protestants, who would have to choose between exile and acceptance of Catholicism thus reformed.[9] Montaigne's views were probably close to those of his friend. On June 12, 1562, he asked to sit with the Paris Parlement and, apparently gladly, made the required formal profession of Catholic faith. Some of his closest friends in the Bordeaux Parlement were Catholic militants. He worked against his sister and brother to see that young Jeanne de Lestonnac was brought up as a Catholic.

His translation of Sebond's *Natural Theology* shows not only his filial piety but also an eagerness to demonstrate the advantages of the Catholic faith. One passage that enlarges so on Sebond as to constitute an actual addition by Montaigne contrasts eloquently the repose and assurance of the dutiful believer with the torment of doubt that plagues those who have strayed.[10]

The *Travel Journal* reveals Montaigne as a dutiful Catholic with great curiosity about religious theory and practice and fondness for theological discussion, especially with Protestants. The papal censor treated him with cordial respect; the Pope helped him become a Roman citizen. He had two meetings with his good friend the emi-

nent Jesuit Juan Maldonado, who according to a younger contemporary, Pierre de Lancre, was "the heart and soul" of Montaigne,
in his opinion the ablest theologian of his time and a sure authority
in religious matters.[11]

A number of letters by, to, and about Montaigne in the last ten
years of his life tally with all the external evidence to reveal him
as a tolerant but firm Catholic loyalist. The likeliest account of his
death, by his friend Estienne Pasquier, shows him as hearing Mass
said in his room as he felt death approaching, and dying as he
raised himself in bed at the elevation of the host. The memorial
tributes by friends show no doubt of his religious sincerity.

Yet Montaigne's religious views and attitudes pose problems for
many readers. Some of these problems are more apparent than
real. For example, to read Montaigne's statement in the "Apology"
(II: 12, 422, S325) *"Nous sommes Chrestiens à mesme titre que nous
sommes ou Perigordins ou Alemans"* ["We are Christians by the
same title that we are Perigordians or Germans"] as a disquietingly
relativistic pronouncement about the societal origins of all religion
is to miss the context, which reveals it as a cry of distress at the accidental reasons that Montaigne finds for the belief of his neighbors.

More serious, especially for Protestants, is what (to put the case
at its worst) one might call the "double-think" involved in the
disclaimer of his merely "human notions" that we noted a few
pages ago. Yet the conviction that philosophy and theology can
lead to different conclusions goes back at least to Duns Scotus and
Occam and was a widely accepted view in Montaigne's time. That
it is a constant in him is attested by other almost identical passages
where he states that his submission is not perfunctory but sincere
and adds: *"Je parle enquerant et ignorant, me rapportant de la
resolution, purement et simplement, aux creances communes et
legitimes. Je n'enseigne poinct, je raconte."* ["I speak as an ignorant
inquirer, referring the decision purely and simply to the common
and authorized beliefs. I do not teach, I tell."] (III: 2, 784, S612; cf.
I: 56, 302–3, S229.) Such a statement made by a man having great
faith in the power of reason might well be suspect; but Montaigne
consistently recognizes his lack of access to absolute truth and the
authority of professionals in theology. The Council of Trent had

laid heavy stress on the discipline of religion, the duty to accept absolutely the dogma and authority of the Church; St. Ignatius of Loyola, founder of the Jesuit order that Montaigne so admired, had pointed up the paradox involved by stating in his *Spiritual Exercises* that if something that appears to us white is affirmed by the Church to be black, we must likewise declare it black. Montaigne's freedom in airing, as part of an honest self-portrait, his own fallible impressions of even theological matters does not mean that he doubted the Church's teachings. *"Ou il faut se submettre du tout,"* he wrote, *"à l'authorité de nostre police ecclesiastique, ou du tout s'en dispenser."* ["We must either submit completely to the authority of our ecclesiastical government, or do without it completely."] (I: 27, 181, S134.) Nothing in his life or works even suggests that he did without it completely.

Another problem is that of his Christian skepticism, or fideism (using this term loosely and anachronistically), by which he not merely shows faith to be beyond reason but seems to found it on the impotence of reason. When, as in a Pascal, faith is an overriding concern, skepticism about man's reason is obviously subordinate to it. This is much less clear in Montaigne, whose view of man is basically comic, not tragic, and who seems to delight, for its own sake, in the act of humbling human reason. But the comparison with Pascal is unfortunate; Pascal is just one type of Christian, extreme in his single-minded rejection of the world. Montaigne is a very different type; everything suggests that his skepticism is intended to set faith, and the authority of the Church, beyond the reach of man's presumptuous and fallible reason.

The "Apology for Raymond Sebond" offers other problems besides skepticism, notably the fact that it is a lame defense if indeed a defense at all. However, as I have noted at length in Chapter IV, I believe this fact is adequately explained by the probable circumstances of its composition (a command performance) and by Montaigne's view of Sebond as a potentially useful worker for the good cause though an unimpressive thinker. That the chapter is mainly a counterattack against one group of Sebond's critics seems to me a sign not that Montaigne was perfidious but that such an attack seemed the best defense for such a vulnerable book.

A more serious problem concerns God and his relation to man.

Montaigne sees God as very remote. In stressing his infinity and man's nullity and putting the knowledge of God's mysteries beyond the reach of human reason, he seems at times—intellectually in the "Apology," morally in "Repentance"—to allow man virtually no chance to rise toward God by his own effort. Moreover, especially in "Repentance," he seems to welcome this remoteness, which allows man to work out his own moral code according to his sense of human nature. Not content with seeing nature as the order of God's creation, Montaigne often seems almost to equate it with God. The code he preaches for good living is based primarily on his sense of human nature and its needs and only incidentally, if at all, on Scripture.

There are some qualifications to be noted. The man whose access to God Montaigne limits or denies is normally man without divine grace—a gift of God which man cannot earn. At least some of his moral pronouncements may have been intended merely to show his practice and illustrate his statement "I do not teach, I tell." The morality he preaches, with its stress on truth, tolerance, and fairness to all, may seem to him a practical selection of the main Christian virtues that govern our dealings with others and keep us from doing them harm. These were badly needed virtues in Montaigne's time; he may have wished to show that even on purely human grounds they led to happiness and man had an inescapable duty to practice them.

Nevertheless, most of these criticisms seem valid and the extenuations insufficient. Montaigne's views in this area appear to be these. His is a rather permissive, *laisser-faire* God, paternally benign for all his remoteness, whose gifts to man of life and of nature are proofs of his kindness to us: *"Tout bon il a faict tout bon."* ["Himself all good, he has made all things good."] (III: 13, 1094, S855.) Nature being good and a good guide to man, God can leave it to man to find his proper place and way in it. Though man is frail and fallible, that is how God created him and meant him to be. God's other main attribute (besides his goodness) is his justice (I: 56, 303, S230), which he exercises more often than his power. Conduct is our primary obligation, the reason we are here (III: 10, 984, S769–70). Montaigne's own conduct, in which theory and practice meet, is more just than that of his French contemporaries, whatever their creed (II: 17, 629, S490; III: 2, 784–85, 790, S612, 616; III: 9, 923, 933–34, 949, S722, 729–30, 742; etc.); it is true to the nature that God willed him to have; he can say with a clear conscience, "I can do no better," since his conscience is content with itself, "not as the conscience of an angel or of a horse, but as the conscience of a man" (III: 2, 784, 791, S612, 617). In short, in his eyes a morality founded on his own clear-sighted sense of justice is thoroughly satisfactory to God.

To sum up. Among the distinguishing marks of Montaigne's religion are strong elements of a general conservatism in motive and of fideism and naturalism in belief;[12] a sturdy independence combined with complete submissiveness to the supreme authority of the Church; an overriding concern with conduct, in which justice is the key virtue. Many of his religious attitudes were sharpened, if not even in some degree formed, by his opposition to Protestantism, not only as an enemy of law and order, but also doctrinally for an excessive, presumptuous trust in the reason of the individual believer and a dangerous minimizing of works to the advantage of faith. Montaigne's formation, though Christian, was that of a layman and above all a humanist; the writers who did most to shape his mind were not the Church Fathers but Seneca, Plutarch, and Plato. In his sense of man and of man's relation to God, the Fall and Redemption do not loom large, nor in his ethics does the Christian stress on love, humility, and the contrite heart; Ecclesiastes seems more congenial to him than the Gospels. Yet most of his ethical values, though unmarked by fervor or saintliness and rarely specifically Christian, seem—as they clearly seemed to him—compatible with Christianity. It is abundantly clear that he was a stanch practicing Catholic in his own eyes and in those of all the contemporaries whose view of him we know. The modern reader may do well, like most scholars today, to accept their view.

~§ IX ह~

THE *ESSAIS*:
CONCEPT AND STRUCTURE

Montaigne was both the first essay writer and the only one who never thought of himself as one. To paraphrase his own words about himself as a philosopher (II: 12, 528, S409), we might call him an unpremeditated and fortuitous essayist.

Then what did he think he *was* doing? Apparently, writing some 107 chapters, divided into three books, the sum of which he called his *Essais*.[1] His title applies to the sum, not seriatim to its parts. For him the *Essais* were not a genre, but, as we have seen, a succession of probings, trials, or samplings, of the self.

Out of his many uses of the term to designate his book, the few that could possibly refer to a genre need not: his statement that "these essays" will probably displease both the learned and the ignorant and find readers only in between (I: 54, 300, S227); his rejection of praise for the language of "these essays," since his rich substance provides material for countless more (I: 40, 245, S184–85); and his sally *"Tel . . . faict des essais, qui ne sauroit faire des effaicts"* ["one man . . . produces essays, who cannot produce results"] (III: 9, 971, S759).

Normally the dominant meaning of tests, trials, or experiments is clear, as when he twice writes of his book as the *essai* of his natural faculties (I: 26, 145, S107), once adding "and not at all of the acquired ones" (II: 10, 387, S296), or speaks of it as the *essais* of his judgment (I: 50, 289, S219; II: 17, 637, S495). These four passages also indicate the relation between his concept of the essay and his plan of self-study. Although, as the first one shows, he counts his judgment among his natural faculties, still basically the "essays of his judgment" reveal the self-portrayer, the "essay of his natural faculties" the self portrayed. And he seems to have found his title only when he found his subject: himself.

In his final writings the sense of *essai* as "sampling" or "trial work" (*coup d'essai*) grows stronger, as when he calls his book nothing but *"un registre des essais de ma vie"* ["a record of the essays of my life"] (III: 13, 1056, S826). Apparently at all times all these meanings—tests or trials, experiments, samplings, trial works—were in his mind and either dominant or latent in his use of the word, but the meaning of a genre was not. His own term for the component parts of his three books is "chapters" (III: 9, 973–74, S761–62; and *passim*); and to be strictly true to his intent, we should refer to them as such.

Yet he left behind a work that (in the plural and in general) he called *Essais* and that gave its name to a literary form practiced by countless writers since. Bacon took the title before—as far as we know—he ever read Montaigne[2] and applied it to a very different genre, terse and didactic; and later practitioners—Cowley, Addison and Steele, Fielding, Johnson, Goldsmith, Lamb, De Quincey, Macaulay, Emerson, Stevenson—made of the genre what the editors of Webster (second edition) wrote of it: "A literary composition, analytical or interpretative in nature, dealing with its subject from a more or less personal standpoint and permitting a considerable freedom of style and method." This is something more methodically analytical, less personal and self-revealing, and much less free, than what Montaigne left behind, which we might describe as a literary form devised by him for self-discovery and self-revelation (and later also for the discovery and revelation of human nature), and hence free and associative in order, since for him no methodical order could probe the self without distorting it. Incidentally, because it was Montaigne who (however unintentionally) created the genre, it has the style his personality gave it—conversational, involving the reader, humorous, concrete, full of image and metaphor—a kind of poetic prose that does not seek to be poetry in prose. Of this, more later.

One of the most striking features of Montaigne's book is the freedom with which he orders his materials: the arrangement of his chapters in relation to each other and of the parts within each chapter. Montaigne stresses this often. His writings, he once says, are only *"crotesques et corps monstrueux, rappiecez de divers membres, sans certaine figure, n'ayants ordre, suite ny proportion que fortuite"* ["grotesques and monstrous bodies, pieced together of divers members, without definite shape, having no order, sequence, or proportion other than accidental"] (I: 28, 181, S135). Elsewhere he writes: *"Je n'ay point d'autre sergent de bande à ranger mes pieces, que la fortune. A mesme que mes resveries se presentent, je les entasse; tantost elles se pressent en foule, tantost elles se trainent à la file. Je veux qu'on voye mon pas naturel et ordinaire, ainsin detraqué qu'il est."* ["I have no other marshal but fortune to arrange my bits. As my fancies present themselves, I pile them up; now they come pressing in a crowd, now dragging single file. I want people to see my natural and ordinary pace, however off the track it is."] (II: 10, 388, S297.) In both these cases, he seems to be speaking of both types of order, among the essays as well as within each one.

Now Montaigne, it is true, like to plume himself on his casualness, on all that distinguishes him from a "maker of books"; yet on this score we do well to pay him heed. Few scholars have had much to say about the order in which Montaigne sets his chapters, for the simple reason, I believe, that there are not many clear-cut things to be said. The novelist Michel Butor has recently made a valiant and fascinating attempt;[3] but when he departs from the few solid indications we have, I often fail to recognize either Montaigne or the *Essais*.

Pierre Villey has shown that the chapters of Books I and II are not arranged in the order of their presentation; and moreover, that although most of Book I was written before most of Book II, there are many exceptions: I: 1, 2, 26, 29, 31, for example, were composed later than II: 1–6 and much of II: 12.

The one explicit pattern in the chapters of Book I (I: 28, 181–82, S135) is Montaigne's placement of those on La Boétie (28: "Of Friendship" and 29: "Twenty-nine Sonnets of Etienne de La Boétie") squarely at the center of the fifty-seven. His original plan was to make I: 28 in particular, and Book I in general, the "grotesque" setting for La Boétie's *Voluntary Servitude*. However, its publication by Protestant subversives in 1574 and 1576 as a tract against monarchy led him to leave it out. In its place he put the new chapter presenting twenty-nine of his friend's sonnets—which he also ultimately deleted on the grounds that they had been published elsewhere.

His two chapters on education are explicitly paired (I: 26, 147, S109) by his statement that a friend who had read the earlier one (I: 25: "Of Pedantry") had urged him to enlarge on the subject "Of the Education of Children" (I: 26). The opening words of Chapter 6 pair it with 5, those of 40 with 39. Unstated pairings are commoner: 3 and 4 on how passions go beyond their primary objects, 19 and 20 on the importance of death.[4]

"Of Idleness" (8) would have made a natural introductory chapter and may have been intended as one; but once Montaigne decided to make himself the subject of his book, he needed "To the Reader" to announce the fact. The definitive Chapter 1 ("By Diverse Means We Arrive at the Same End"), by presenting man as a vain, diverse, and undulating object on which it is hard to found any constant and uniform judgment, is a natural introduction both to Book I and to the two books of the original *Essais* of 1580.

Book II, as we noted, was written mainly later than Book I. Though chapters 1–6 date from Montaigne's early retirement, about three-quarters of the total of thirty-seven (7–11, 16–37) seem to belong to the years 1578–80, just before publication. Nowhere in Book II does Montaigne give any clue to the ordering of the chapters. The numerical center is the treatment of Julian the Apostate in "The Liberty of Conscience" (19); but to make that chapter therefore, as Butor does, the center of gravity of the book, and the book an apology of paganism, is to misread Montaigne badly.

The dominant chapter is clearly the "Apology for Raymond Sebond" (II: 12), almost half the book in length and almost five times as long as any other chapter in the first two books. Butor argues that Montaigne places it near but before the center of the book to make it central to both I and I–II combined. If indeed its placement was important to Montaigne, his reasons may well have been very different, if not opposite. He so often contradicts or modifies some of the main views expressed in the "Apology"[5] that I suspect he wanted the chapter to be neither the center nor the conclusion of either Book II or Books I–II, but rather a strong statement of the skeptical position and an important stage on his way to self-study and self-revelation.

Many of the chapters form a rather clear chronological pattern: critique of Stoical humanism preparing the way for the "Apology" (2–3); the "Apology" itself (12); critique of certain aspects of the "Apology" (parts of 8, 11, 12 itself, 29); preparation for self-study as a natural consequence of the "Apology"'s critique of our knowledge of externals (parts of 6, 12); self-study, reliance on self, self-portrayal (17–18); and (37) the philosophy of the free man with nothing to fear.

Virtually central in Book II is a cluster of three chapters (16–18) which Montaigne presents as composed consecutively: "Of Glory," "Of Presumption," and "Of Giving the Lie." The second of these offers Montaigne's first self-portrait; it and the third seek to prove that self-portrayal is justifiable and no proof of presumption. Thus they are central to Montaigne's late-found plan of making himself the subject of his book.

Two other linkages are striking: Chapters 33 and 34 by their concern with Julius Caesar, 35 and 36 by their treatment of three good wives and the three most outstanding men.

Despite the rather optimistic chronological movement just noted, Montaigne ends the book as he had begun it, on the theme of human diversity. His opening chapter had pronounced us as different from ourselves as from others; his final chapter—and with it not only Book II but the *Essais* of 1580—ends on the variety of human opinions with the words "diversity and discordance." [6]

In Book III the nearest thing to a pattern is that the chapters seem arranged in the order of their composition. [7] The only one whose place appears unchangeable is the last, "Of Experience" (13), whose final pages form a triumphant conclusion to Book III and the entire *Essais*. A good introductory chapter would have been the second ("Of Repentance"), with its new awareness of unity in the individual and in mankind; but its bold moral stance in a sensitive religious area may have suggested a less conspicuous place. For that matter, Chapter 1, "Of the Useful and the Honorable," makes a satisfactory introduction to a book much concerned with the superiority of private morality to public, of the honorable to the expedient. Central numerically but in no other way is Chapter 7, "Of the Disadvantage of Greatness."

All in all, the arrangement of Montaigne's chapters in each book and in the work as a whole reveals several minor patterns but no overall pattern except the working of the same freely associative mind that reveals itself also in the ordering of each chapter.

The individual chapters are extremely varied in form and movement, partly because Montaigne's mind had many movements, and partly because he had to write his way into full possession of the medium he created. What follows is a sampling of different types, each studied in its original form.[8]

Most of Montaigne's earliest chapters are short; many are rather impersonal. "One Is Punished for Defending a Place Obstinately without Reason" (I: 15) is about a page long. Montaigne notes that valor, like other virtues, has its limits; which explains his chapter title. He illustrates his point with three examples, points out that the test of a reasonable defense is subjective, and ends by noting that some leaders consider any defense against themselves unreasonable.

Also short but much more personal is "Of Idleness" (I: 8), composed of two similes and an example. Montaigne compares unseeded lands and unimpregnated women with idle minds, then cites as an example his own mind, which when left idle gave birth to such fantastic monsters that, to study their ineptitude at leisure, he has begun to keep a record of them. The chapter is clearly preplanned, with the movement of a well-constructed sentence; but Montaigne seems to relish his well-contrived similes, and metaphor abounds as he seeks to express his problem. Though his flight is short, he is trying his wings.

A more complex early chapter, "That to Philosophize Is to Learn to Die" (I: 20), treats a personal problem with a mosaic of quotations and reminiscences from such ancients as Lucretius, Horace, Seneca, and Cicero. Montaigne starts by quoting Cicero to justify his title; offers two interpretations of the quotation; and goes on to develop the second: that the aim of wisdom and reason must be to teach us to die, since our contentment, which they must surely seek, depends on our freedom from the fear of death. After discussing and illustrating this theme, he asks why we should worry about death, and answers that unpreparedness costs too much. He himself has always lived with the thought of death. Though we ought —and he hopes—to be active to the end, we must await it everywhere. Nature will help us to put our own death in its place by pointing out that to live at all is to live enough, since life repeats itself; that it is only fair to give way to others; that life is the road to death; and so on. In conclusion, Montaigne wonders why death seems easy to many ordinary folk, and decides that we make it hard by its trappings and would be better off without them.

In the next-earliest chapters, composed around 1573–75, we find Montaigne experimenting with new types. One of these is the about-face (possibly derived from Plato's *Lysis*) in which he starts in one direction and then reverses his field. In "Drunkenness" (II: 2), for example, he begins by pronouncing this "a gross and brutish vice" (322, S245), but goes on to seem to condone it by pointing to examples of the mildness with which many ancients regarded it. A later chapter, "Of Cruelty" (II: 11), proclaims at first that virtue requires difficulty and conflict and illustrates this view for a couple of pages, only to remark "I have come this far quite at my ease" (402, S308) and then point out that the virtue of Socrates must have been beyond conflict or even temptation to vice.

A striking earlier example is "A Custom of the Island of Cea" (II: 3; 1573–75). Since Christianity forbids suicide, Montaigne opens with a deprecatory statement that he is merely playing the fool and following his fancies, and that the decision in such matters rests with the authority of the divine will. As we have noted already (p. 24), for about two pages he cites, with apparent approval, words and deeds showing suicide as the one sure remedy for human ills. Then he turns abruptly to the arguments against suicide: that it is for God alone to give us leave to depart when He will, that suicide is a cowardly escape from pain, which it is braver to endure, and that by its disdain for life it is ridiculous and unnatural. After two pages on this theme he turns for six to the situations in which philosophy has judged suicide permissible, thus keeping the logic of his movement while giving it the appearance of an *S* curve; and with these he comes to the custom of his title and the end of his chapter.

In all three of these chapters, if I read him rightly, his opening position is one he had once held but then abandoned; the technique he has found for presenting this fact not only dramatically advances two opposite points of view one after the other, but also reveals the change in his thinking over a stretch of time. By showing the order as well as the substance of his thought, it adumbrates the movement of his final chapters.

Another rather early chapter, "Of Practice" (II: 6; 1573–74), shows Montaigne for the first time drawing conclusions from an experience of his own—his fall from his horse—about death and self-study. In its original form (for the final pages were added after 1588) it discussed approaches to death, related his closest one, and drew conclusions: that we exaggerate death in anticipation, and that each man can teach himself much by studying himself closely.

Even as he reaches out in the mid-1570's toward freer forms of association, Montaigne always adapts his structure to his aims. His "Apology for Raymond Sebond" is an all-out attack on human vanity and presumption. Accordingly, though it is often free and associative in detail, its overall structure (as we noted above, pp. 28–29) has the tightness and logic needed to make it the powerful weapon that it is.

Typical of the chapters of 1578–80 is what we might call the rather long "essay as treatise" in which Montaigne deals straightforwardly but freely with his subject. Under this rubric I would list "Of the Education of Children" (I: 26), "Of the Affection of Fathers for Their Children" (II: 8), "Of Books" (II: 10), "Of Presumption" (II: 17), and "Of the Resemblance of Children to Fathers" (II: 37).

The second of these (II: 8) begins with a deprecatory account of his project; claims that a true self-portrait must show his admiration for the addressee, the exemplary widow and mother Louise d'Estissac; urges that parents regard their children with a rational, not merely instinctive, affection; and goes on to a long account of parent-child relations, advising parents to cultivate fairness and seek to win their children's love, not fear. "Of Books" (II: 10) also starts with a modest account of Montaigne's aim and plan, tells of the two kinds of books he likes (those that entertain him, those that teach him to live and die well), discusses examples of each kind (and one author, Cicero, whom he reads but does not like), and concludes with three samples of his judgments of books written in them after a careful reading.

In "Presumption" (II: 17) Montaigne denies that this vice is implicit in self-portrayal, distinguishes two aspects of it—overestimation of self and underestimation of others—admits that he tends to rate mankind rather low, but says it would be hard for anyone to esteem him less than he esteems himself (II: 17, 618, S481). In the self-portrait that follows, the one quality he claims is judgment (640, S498; in later editions "sense"—cf. DB II, 235), which everyone else claims too. Returning to esteem for others, he admits that he has known of few men who even come close to the great ancients; on that score he may be guilty of presumption.

The title "Of the Resemblance of Children to Fathers" (II: 37) anticipates Book III by announcing not the main theme of the chapter but the link between it and the next theme in importance. Montaigne begins with the changes that his book already reveals in himself; notes one change that the years have brought him, the kidney stone; tells how a year and a half of its agonizing pain, by proving milder than he had anticipated, has left him surprisingly content to be alive; and wonders how this hereditary malady lay dormant so long—as it had with his father—in his kidneys. Heredity and illness lead him to his main subject, his inherited mistrust of medicine. He defends this attitude in a long account of the shortcomings of medicine, showing acutely what a vast accumulation of experiment it would need to become a science. He concludes by addressing Madame de Duras about his project, his concern to fashion his life and not merely make books, and then saying that others may have equally strong reasons for defending medicine, since the most intrinsic quality of human opinions is their diversity and discordance.

Of these five examples of "the essay as treatise," the one that most anticipates the freedom of Book III is "Of the Education of Children" (I: 26). Montaigne opens by saying that he never knew a father to disavow his son for any deformity; thus he will not disown this ignorant brainchild of his; unlike many authors' books, it is at least his own. It presents only his opinions; and at a friend's suggestion he will offer the Countess of Gurson, who is soon to give birth, surely to a boy, one unusual notion he has about education.

This "one notion" seems to be the entire theme of the chapter: to form the judgment, not just the memory, and thus make of the child a morally responsible man. Montaigne first discusses the tutor, who should exemplify character and understanding even more than learning; then proper teaching, by discussion not inculcation, training the child to be his own judge of everything. The test of his lesson is the course of his life. He can learn from every experience; the world is to be his book. Travel will teach him perspective in space, history in time. Physical training will make his body tough and adaptable. Versatile and free, he will do good because he likes to. Since learning Latin and Greek in the usual way is long and tedious, Montaigne tells how his father had him taught Latin without tears, as a first language, almost from the cradle. He concludes that unless we arouse affection for learning, we will produce mere book-laden donkeys; for we must not merely lodge learning in us but espouse it.

Amid all this we find observations on Montaigne's love of history and poetry; writers' borrowings that only show up their own poverty; the power of natural inclinations; the value of silence and modesty; the comic limits of our perspective; the beauty and worth of true (that is to say, moral) philosophy; the difference between a grammarian or logician and a gentleman; the futility of sophistic arguments; and the style Montaigne loves. While he gives the chapter clear movement and order, Montaigne still manages to touch on a host of subjects related in his mind to education.

Book III offers, as Montaigne tells us, a freer order than did the first two: his ideas, as he says, follow one another sometimes only from a distance; but it is the inattentive reader who loses his subject, not he himself. He wants the matter to make its own divisions, without his needing to write glosses on himself; and now, by the greater length and complexity of his chapters, he requires more attention of the reader. What he likes, as he says, is "the poetic gait, by leaps and gambols" (III: 9, 973-74, S761-62).

The chapter in which Montaigne makes these remarks, "Of Vanity" (III: 9), is a good example of his greater freedom. A distinguished Montaigne scholar early in this century, Grace Norton, even argued that it must have been composed out of two separate original chapters, one on travel and the other on vanity. However, as other critics have rightly noted since,[9] it deserves its title: vanity is indeed its dominant theme. Montaigne illustrates it wth examples of vanity from his own life: at the outset (922, S721), that of writing about it so vainly; throughout the chapter (925–67, S723–56), the insatiable craving for novelty, for whatever is not at hand, that keeps him ever on the move; and in conclusion (978–79, S764–66) his struggle to get, and delight to have, an "authentic bull of Roman citizenship." [10] But in Montaigne's eyes these are minor vanities. Of his craving for novelty he writes: " *'Il y a de la vanité, dictes vous, en cet amusement.'—Mais où non? Et ces beaux preceptes sont vanité, et vanité toute la sagesse.*" [" 'There is vanity,' you say, 'in this amusement.' But where is there not? And these fine precepts are vanity, and all wisdom is vanity."] (967, S756.)

If all is vanity, there may be much to be said in defense of Montaigne. Vanity itself is not as bad as the prevalent corruption. Among the countless vanities that are as vain or as bad as his—or more so—are reform in dress when the state is falling apart; loving whatever is your own better than what is anyone else's, like Montaigne's friend with the chamber pots; worrying too much about your household affairs; affecting a "philosophic" disdain for those affairs; spending time studying your money; worrying about the ideal state, when you have to deal with men as they are; trying to reform the state without knowing that you can make it better; despairing over the state, which is hard to shatter; thinking that age normally brings wisdom; craving to see only Frenchmen and live only French style when abroad; thinking we possess things—and people—only when they are at hand; wanting others to suffer from our own suffering and death; and above all (967–70, 974, S756–58, 762), setting up moral theories that we have no intention of living up to, that are not fit for man.

If all is vanity, it is important how individual vanities affect us. Montaigne readily admits that *"je m'emploie à faire valoir la vanité mesme et l'asnerie si elle m'apporte du plaisir."* ["I apply myself to make use of vanity itself, and asininity, if it brings me any pleasure."] (974–75, S762.) Finally, if all is vanity, perhaps what matters

most is whether we are aware of it. As Montaigne says in his conclusion, *"ceux qui le sentent en ont un peu meilleur compte, encore ne sçay-je"* ["those who are aware of it are a little better off—
though I don't know"]; and *"C'est tousjours vanité pour toy, dedans
et dehors, mais elle est moins vanité quand elle est moins estendue."*
["It is always vanity for you, within and without; but it is less vanity when it is less extensive."] (979–80, S766.)

This long chapter includes many serious ideas besides those on
vanity: the ugly plight of France; the book; the pressure of obligation; Montaigne's love of Paris and Rome; the value of friendship
and the bereavement he feels with his friend gone; his preference
for a casual death that will not involve others; his gratitude to
Fortune for not treating him harshly; the inevitability of moral
compromise in public life; and the unexpected normative value
of self-portrayal. Self-portrayal is everywhere in the chapter, but is
always subordinate to—and at times an example of—the overriding
theme of human vanity.

A somewhat similar but shorter chapter is "Of Repentance" (III:
2), which Montaigne opens with the theme of the constancy of flux;
studs with crucial statements like those of the unity of the individual and the race, the greater value, appropriateness, and rigor of
private than of public life; and fills with examples of the many
counterfeits—superficial reform, regret, aging, and the like—that
too often pass for repentance. The chapter is at the same time a
self-portrait of Montaigne as moralist, in which his findings about
his own and human nature form the basis for his independent morality.

Another rich chapter of Book III, in which Montaigne combines
epistemology with morality, psychology, and self-portrayal, is his
long last one, "Of Experience" (III: 13). Experience is the dominant theme, but Montaigne studies it in many aspects, and many
other things in relation to it. He starts by considering it and reason
as aids in man's restless search for knowledge; shows how the multiplicity and diversity of phenomena weaken its power, and how man
multiplies this multiplicity by his zest for interpretation, in literature, religion, and the law. After an excursus on the injustice of
justice, Montaigne turns to his favorite subject, self-study, which
he calls his metaphysics and his physics (1050, S821), and the help

it gives us: not only to amend our conduct, but to gain insight into others. A rather contorted transition—"this . . . is nothing but a record of the essays of my life"; my spiritual life is exemplary only in reverse, as a horrible example; but my bodily health, "not at all corrupted or altered by art or theorizing," can serve others as "useful experience" (1056, S826)—leads to the bulk of the chapter, Montaigne's physical regimen and what experience has taught him in this regard. Then the last ten pages (1086–97, S849–57) offer the fruits of Montaigne's experience: that we should live our life appropriately, as beings whom God created part body and part soul, gratefully enjoying in harmony the legitimate pleasures of both our natural parts.

Not all Montaigne's chapters are so straightforward. There are some, as he says (III: 9, 973, S761), whose titles do not "embrace their matter" but "only denote it by some sign." The classic example is "Of Coaches" [11] (III: 6), where Montaigne's associative links are often tenuous and hard to follow. He starts by saying that great authors often adduce specious causes whose truth they themselves doubt; witness Plutarch's theory that seasickness is caused by fear. Though experience has proven this false for Montaigne, he can ill abide a coach, or any other transportation but horseback; and the uneven movement of a boat on water troubles his stomach and head. From this he turns to strange ancient conveyances: chariots drawn by lions, tigers, stags, naked women, or ostriches; then back to a host of other lavish Roman spectacles. This leads him to our inferiority to the great ancients, "even in these vanities" (885, S692); and this to the sad fact that modern Europeans, not the ancient Greeks or Romans, have discovered and conquered the New World (886–88, S693–95). Montaigne's ensuing indictment of the Europeans (especially Spaniards) in the New World for their treachery, avarice, and cruelty is so eloquent and sustained as to constitute the heart of the chapter. However, one explicit reminder leads him back to *"la pompe et magnificence, par où je suis entré en ce propos"* ["pomp and magnificence, whereby I entered upon this subject"] (893, S698); he proclaims Peru a match in this respect even for Greece, Rome, or Egypt; then another reminder, *"Retombons à nos coches"* ["Let us fall back to our coaches"], brings him back to Peruvian forms of transport and thus in conclusion to his announced subject.

Chapters such as this one—and possibly "Of Cripples" or "Of Physiognomy" [12]—display a virtuosity that may seem almost coquettish. For me at least, their order is not as effective as the more predictable order of "Vanity," "Repentance," or "Experience." They do show, however, how far Montaigne is willing to go from the beaten track in essaying the limits of free association in his newly created genre.

It often seems as though by the time he wrote Book III Montaigne might have trained himself to let his mind associate freely for a while, then to recapture the track it had followed, note this down, and make this the order of a chapter he filled out at leisure. Though pure conjecture, it might just explain his order—or at least how he achieved it.

❧ X ❧

STYLE

For two centuries after his death, admirers of Montaigne's style, though sometimes great—Pascal, Montesquieu, Diderot—were a small minority; the consensus, especially in neoclassicist France (less so in England), found him crude, disorderly, and quaint. The Romantics, however, though they disliked his ironic temper, hailed the stylist for his freedom, vigor, concreteness, and allegiance to nature against art. Chateaubriand, Mme. de Staël, Stendhal, George Sand, Michelet, Mérimée delighted in his style; Flaubert compared its succulence to that of a ripe fruit; Sainte-Beuve reveled in its tireless flow of vivid images; in America, Emerson called Montaigne's the least *written* of books and marveled: "Cut these words, and they would bleed; they are vascular and alive." [1]

In the century and a quarter since Sainte-Beuve and Emerson, Montaigne's style has been recognized as one of his greatest qualities —by some, as his greatest. Studies have proliferated.[2] Some have stressed his use of asyndeton and his creatural realism; some his Atticism, his preference for the crisp, disjointed Senecan style to the orotund Ciceronian; some his play on words, which is often the despair of the translator; some, diversely but persuasively, his baroque qualities. All these are indeed aspects of Montaigne's style. As most outstanding I would myself list four—none fully exclusive of the others or of those just mentioned—on which nearly all critics agree. First, the movement and flux, the pre-Bergsonian "mobilism," that Montaigne finds all about him and reflects in his order and his metaphors (Thibaudet, Buffum, Gray, Starobinski; see footnote 2). Second, the fondness for paradox and the ironic temper that— despite his earnestness—informs his entire work (Auerbach, Buffum,

Samaras). Third, his conversational tone and manner (virtually all critics). Fourth, the living concreteness of his imagery (all critics).

A careful craftsman, as his corrections on the Bordeaux Copy show, Montaigne is in the main a perceptive judge of his own style. He seems sincere, however, in taking a disparaging view of it, largely because of his nominalistic concern for substance (the reality behind the mask) and his Spartan-nobiliary concern with deeds, not words.

> *Je veux que les choses surmontent et qu'elles remplissent de façon l'imagination de celuy qui escoute, qu'il n'aye aucune souvenance des mots. . . .* (I: 26, 171, S127.)
>
> *Tout est grossier chez moy; il y a faute de gentillesse et de beauté . . . Ma façon n'ayde rien à la matiere. Voilà pourquoy il me la faut forte, qui aye beaucoup de prise et qui luise d'elle mesme.* (II: 17, 620, S483.)
>
> [I want the substance to stand out, and so to fill the imagination of the listener that he will have no memory of the words. . . .
>
> Everything I write is crude; it lacks distinction and beauty. . . . My fashioning is no help to the matter. That is why I need my matter strong, with plenty of grip, and shining by its own light.]

He is proud of the richness of his substance (I: 40, 245, S185), since for him, as for the Pléiade poets, it is the things that count, not the words. When he reads a rich passage in a great author, he comments: *"je ne dicts pas que c'est bien dire, je dicts que c'est bien penser."* ["I do not say 'This is well said,' I say 'This is well thought.' "] (III: 5, 850, S665.)

Generally, however, he shows a good sense of his own style. Here he is on his movement: *"J'ayme l'alleure poetique, à sauts et à gambades. . . . Je vais au change, indiscrettement et tumultuairement. Mon style et mon esprit vont vagabondant de mesmes."* ["I love the poetic gait, by leaps and gambols. . . . I seek out change indiscriminately and tumultuously. My style and my mind alike go roaming."] (III: 9, 973, S761.) Both ironic temper and conversational tone are suggested when he writes: *"J'ay naturellement un style comique et privé"* ["I have naturally a humorous and familiar style"] (I: 40, 246, S186). The oral quality, vigor and savor, free order, and naturalness appear in this account of his favorite style:

*Le parler que j'ayme, c'est un parler simple et naïf, tel sur le papier
qu'à la bouche; un parler succulent et nerveux, court et serré, non tant
delicat et peigné comme vehement et brusque . . . plustost difficile
qu'ennuieux, esloingné d'affectation, desreglé, descousu et hardy;
chaque lopin y face son corps; non pedantesque, non fratesque, non
pleideresque, mais plustost soldatesque . . .* (I: 26, 171, S127.)

[The speech I love is a simple, natural speech, the same on paper as in
the mouth; a speech succulent and sinewy, brief and compressed, not
so much dainty and well-combed as vehement and brusque . . . rather
difficult than boring, remote from affectation, irregular, disconnected
and bold; each bit making a body in itself; not pedantic, not monkish,
not lawyer-like, but rather soldierly.]

The most striking of Montaigne's statements about his style shows
his awareness of criticisms that may be made of it and his firm
determination to make form as well as content contribute to a true
self-portrait:

*Je l'eusse faict meilleur ailleurs, mais l'ouvrage eust esté moins mien;
et sa fin principale et perfection, c'est d'estre exactement mien. Je cor-
rigerois bien une erreur accidentale, dequoy je suis plein, ainsi que je
cours inadvertemment; mais les imperfections qui sont en moy ordi-
naires et constantes, ce seroit trahison de les oster. Quand on m'a dit
ou que moy-mesme me suis dict: "Tu es trop espais en figures. Voilà
un mot du creu de Gascoingne. Voilà une frase dangereuse (je n'en
refuis aucune de celles qui s'usent emmy les rues françoises; ceux qui
veulent combatre l'usage par la grammaire se moquent). Voilà un
discours ignorant. Voilà un discours paradoxe. En voilà un trop fol.
Tu te joues souvent; on estimera que tu dies à droit ce que tu dis à
feinte.—Oui, fais-je; mais je corrige les fautes d'inadvertence, non celles
de coustume. Est-ce pas ainsi que je parle par tout? me represente-je
pas vivement? suffit! J'ay faict ce que j'ay voulu: tout le monde me
reconnoit en mon livre, et mon livre en moy."* (III: 5, 853, S667.)

[I would have done it better elsewhere, but the work would have been
less my own; and its principal end and perfection is to be precisely
my own. I would indeed correct an accidental error, and I am full of
them, since I run on carelessly. But the imperfections that are ordinary
and constant in me it would be treachery to remove.

When I have been told, or have told myself: "You are too thick in
figures of speech. Here is a word of Gascon vintage. Here is a dangerous phrase." (I do not avoid any of those that are used in the streets
of France; those who would combat usage with grammar make fools of
themselves.) "This is ignorant reasoning. This is paradoxical reasoning. This one is too mad. You are often playful: people will think you
are speaking in earnest when you are making believe." "Yes," I say,

"but I correct the faults of inadvertence, not those of habit. Isn't this the way I speak everywhere? Don't I represent myself to the life? Enough, then. I have done what I wanted. Everyone recognizes me in my book, and my book in me."

Montaigne's mobilism, his sense of movement everywhere, is manifest in his use of images of movement, notably of walking and flight, and of images ever *in* movement, leading the reader from one to the next. Both aspects, as well as his love of metaphor, appear in the following passage:

> *Il m'advint l'autre jour de tomber sur un tel passage. J'avois trainé languissant après des parolles Françoises si exangues, si descharnées et si vuides de matiere et de sens que ce n'estoient voirement que parolles Françoises; au bout d'un long et ennuyeux chemin, je vins à rencontrer une piece haute, riche et eslevée jusques aux nuës. Si j'eusse trouvé la pente douce et la montée un peu alongée, cela eust esté excusable; c'estoit un precipice si droit et si coupé que, des six premieres paroles, je conneuz que je m'envolois en l'autre monde. De là je descouvris la fondriere d'où je venois, si basse et si profonde, que je n'eus onques plus le cœur de m'y ravaler. Si j'estoffois l'un de mes discours de ces riches despouilles, il esclaireroit par trop la bestise des autres. (I: 26, 145–46, S108.)*

[I happened the other day to come upon such a passage. I had dragged along languidly after French words so bloodless, fleshless, and empty of matter and sense that they really were nothing but French words. At the end of a long and tedious road I came upon a bit that was sublime, rich, and lofty as the clouds. If I had found the slope gentle and the climb a bit slower, it would have been excusable; but it was a precipice so straight and steep that after the first six words I realized that I was flying off into another world. From there I saw the bog I had come out of, so low and deep that I never again had the stomach to go back down into it. If I stuffed one of my chapters with these rich spoils, it would show up too clearly the stupidity of the others.]

It is characteristic of Montaigne's movement that his phrases, sentences, and paragraphs[3] are not like building blocks forming some stately but static edifice; rather they seem to flow, to come tumbling out in an uneven line, like a waterfall—or a living creature: witness his remarks (p. 88) on the speech he likes.

Irony and paradox are apparent not only in Montaigne's content but in all kinds of stylistic habits, notably the abruptness and surprise of syllepsis, oxymoron, and word-play in general. Irony and word-play appear in Montaigne's remark about people who go whoring after the causes of things without first verifying the things themselves: *"Ils laissent là les choses, et s'amusent à traiter les causes. Plaisans causeurs."* ["They leave aside the cases and amuse themselves treating the causes. Comical prattlers!"] (III: 11, 1003, S785.) In "Cannibals," an eloquent discussion of their virtues and native sagacity and of the "civilized" barbarity that is so much worse than theirs leads to Montaigne's ironic conclusion: *"Tout cela ne va pas trop mal: mais quoy, ils ne portent point de haut de chausses!"* ["All this is not too bad; but what of it? They don't wear breeches."] (I: 31, 213, S159.)

The spoken flavor so notable in Montaigne's writing has several overlapping purposes—involvement of the reader, spontaneity, fidelity to the movement of his thought, and thus faithful self-portrayal—and many aspects. He is fond of apparently improvised sentences, where he seems to jump in head first and then work his way out.[4] Long, rambling sentences—too long to quote here—sometimes seem to result from a kind of absentminded agglomeration (II: 36, 732–34, S571–72; III: 5, 832–33, S649–50). On the other hand, the conclusion of the following sentence shows his fondness for crisp verbless phrases, not usual in written style: *"Ils vont, ils viennent, ils trottent, ils dansent, de mort nulles nouvelles."* ["They go, they come, they trot, they dance, of death no news."] (I: 20, 84, S59.)

The same final phrase, set off neither by a conjunction nor by any special punctuation, illustrates Montaigne's fondness for asyndeton, that suppression of connectives that Auerbach shows so well in the opening pages of "Repentance." While by no means peculiar to the spoken word, asyndeton—at least in Montaigne's apparently unpremeditated form—is probably commoner there than in writing. It is also, like dialogue, a device involving the reader by obliging him to fill in the missing connectives.

Dialogue abounds in the *Essais*. When Montaigne reports it, he normally does so directly, keeping it vivid and dramatic; and often what might be expressed as thought is dramatized as speech:

J'accuse merveilleusement cette vitieuse forme d'opiner: "Il est de la Ligue, car il admire la grace de Monsieur de Guise." "L'activité du Roy de Navarre l'estonne: il est Huguenot." "Il treuve cecy à dire aux mœurs du Roy: il est seditieux en son cœur." (III: 10, 990, S774–75.)

[I condemn extraordinarily this bad form of arguing: "He is of the League, for he admires the grace of Monsieur de Guise." "The activity of the king of Navarre amazes him: he is a Huguenot." "He finds this to criticize in the king's morals: he is seditious in his heart."]

When Montaigne speaks for himself, he loves to move from his usual monologue into dialogue: with an addressee (II: 12, 453, S349), with the reader, with an imaginary third party, with mankind, with himself—or with some part of himself.

Only rarely does he address the reader as reader, as when he writes: *"Laisse, lecteur, courir encore ce coup d'essay et ce troisiesme alongeail du reste des pieces de ma peinture."* ["Reader, let this essay of myself run on, and this third extension of the other parts of my painting."] (III: 9, 941, S736.) But he loves to bring him implicitly into the discussion, as in this passage:

Pourquoy, estimant un homme, l'estimez vous tout enveloppé et empaqueté? . . . C'est le pris de l'espée que vous cherchez, non de la guaine . . . Mesurez le sans ses eschaces; qu'il mette à part ses richesses et honneurs, qu'il se presente en chemise. A il le corps propre à ses functions, sain et allegre? Quelle ame a il? (I: 42, 251, S190.)

[Why in judging a man do you judge him all wrapped up in a package? . . . It is the worth of the blade that you seek to know, not of the scabbard . . . Measure him without his stilts; let him put aside his riches and honors, let him present himself in his shirt. Has he a body fit for its functions, healthy and blithe? What sort of soul has he?]

Montaigne likes to show himself in dialogue with various of his parts. Here he is setting his mind to counseling—and trying to cozen—his imagination:

Or je trete mon imagination le plus doucement que je puis . . . Il la faut secourir et flatter, et piper qui peut. Mon esprit est propre à ce service . . .

Vous en plaict-il un exemple? Il dict que c'est pour mon mieux que j'ay la gravele . . .

"La creinte de ce mal, faict-il, t'effraioit autresfois, quand il t'estoit incogneu . . . On n'a point à se plaindre des maladies qui partagent loyallement le temps avec la santé." (III: 13, 1068-71, S836-37.)

[Now I treat my imagination as gently as I can . . . We must help it and flatter it, and fool it if we can. My mind is suited to this service . . .

Would you like an example? It says that it is for my own good that I have the stone . . .

"Fear of this disease," says my mind, "used to terrify you, when it was unknown to you . . . We have no cause for complaint about illnesses that divide the time fairly with health."]

Often the dialogue is with an unnamed party, sometimes with mankind in general, as in the passage quoted above, p. 59. A favorite of mine is the following example of the constant inner dialogue of the self-portrayer, where Montaigne starts with a spontaneous statement, then, because it is mildly self-laudatory, corrects it with self-depreciating irony, and finally takes himself aside and says in effect: No; let's say what we honestly think.

J'aurai eslancé quelque subtilité en escrivant. J'entans bien: mornée pour un autre, affilée pour moy. Laissons toutes ces honestetez. Cela se dict par chacun selon sa force. (I: 10, 42, S27.)
[I will have tossed off some subtle remark as I write. I mean, of course, dull for anyone else, sharp for me. Let's leave aside all these amenities. Each man states this kind of thing according to his powers.]

As this passage shows, Montaigne's alternation between different roles in his book often lends a particular movement to his style. Self-portrayal alone is never quite enough for him; by nature a *moraliste*, he must judge. His statement in "Repentance" *"Je n'enseigne poinct, je raconte"* ["I do not teach, I tell"] (III: 2, 784, S612) is only partly true; less than a page later he is busy teaching:

Les autres ne vous voyent poinct; ils vous devinent par conjectures incertaines . . . Par ainsi ne vous tenez pas à leur sentence; tenez vous à la vostre. (785, S613.)
[Others do not see you, they guess at you by uncertain conjectures . . . Therefore do not cling to their judgment; cling to your own.]

The same movement from disarming self-portrayal to firm prescription is evident in the early pages of "The Education of Children" (I: 26, 148–51, S110–12) when Montaigne passes from the "single fancy" he has to offer on the subject, the preferential alternatives (rather character and understanding than even learning in the tutor, rather a well-made than a well-filled head), and the mild statements of what he would like to see ("I should like the tutor to correct this practice," and so on), to the exclusive alternatives and flat imperatives of the moralist: "I don't want him to think and talk alone, I want him to listen to his pupil . . ." "Let

him be asked for an account . . . Let him be made to show . . .
Let this variety of ideas be set before him; he will choose if he
can; if not, he will remain in doubt . . ."

The most striking aspect of Montaigne's style is his unquench-
able imagery. "His style," Sainte-Beuve wrote, "is a perpetual figure,
renewed at every step; you receive his ideas only in images." [5]
Montaigne creates a world of images that generate other images
and a movement of their own. The form they take is rarely the
simile, almost always the bold poetic metaphor.

Various classifications have been attempted: Thibaudet finds images of movement the commonest, followed by those contrasting
surface with interior; for Baraz the main factor is the body; all
three types are indeed prominent. For Baraz (again) Montaigne's
imagery represents his desire not so much to know nature as to be
in harmony with it. It is not merely a quest of poetic vividness,
though it is partly that; important also is Montaigne's sense of
harmonious correspondence between the material and the im-
material, and his insistence that the physical must have its due.
His is not an incapacity for abstraction, but a happy incapacity
for expressing it other than concretely.

Like many similes, Montaigne's are often rather elaborate, more
calculated and self-conscious than his metaphors, though equally
true to the things they describe. Here is one of his finest:

> *Il est advenu aux gens véritablement sçavans ce qui advient aux espics
> de bled: ils vont s'eslevant et se haussant, la teste droite et fiere, tant
> qu'ils sont vuides; mais, quand ils sont pleins et grossis de grain en
> leur maturité, ils commencent à s'humilier et à baisser les cornes.
> Pareillement, les hommes ayant tout essayé et tout sondé, n'ayant
> trouvé en cet amas de science et provision de tant de choses diverses
> rien de massif et de ferme, et rien que vanité, ils ont renoncé à leur
> presomption et reconneu leur condition naturelle.* (II: 12, 480, S370.)

> [To really learned men has happened what happens to ears of wheat:
> they rise high and lofty, heads erect and proud, as long as they are
> empty; but when they are full and swollen with grain in their ripe-
> ness, they begin to grow humble and lower their horns. Similarly,
> men who have tried everything and sounded everything, having found
> in that pile of knowledge and store of so many various things nothing
> solid and firm, and nothing but vanity, have renounced their presump-
> tion and recognized their natural condition.]

While simile is rather rare in Montaigne, metaphor is everywhere
—even in the simile just quoted—and with it that agent of concrete
vividness, personification.

> *Quant aux facultez naturelles qui sont en moy, dequoy c'est icy l'essay,*
> *je les sens flechir sous la charge. Mes conceptions et mon jugement ne*
> *marche qu'à tastons, chancelant, bronchant et chopant; et quand je*
> *suis allé le plus avant que je puis, si ne suis-je aucunement satisfaict;*
> *je voy encore du païs au delà, mais d'une veuë trouble et en nuage,*
> *que je ne puis desmeler.* (I: 26, 145, S107.)

> [As for the natural faculties that are in me, of which this book is the
> essay, I feel them bending under the load. My conceptions and my
> judgment move only by groping, staggering, stumbling, and blunder-
> ing; and when I have gone ahead as far as I can, still I am not at all
> satisfied: I can still see country beyond, but with a dim and clouded
> vision, so that I cannot clearly distinguish it.] [6]

Personification in Montaigne extends to the embodiment of ideas
or attitudes in persons or creatures: lack of perspective in his village
priest, who, when the vines freeze, infers God's wrath upon the
human race (I: 26, 156, S116); lack of proper self-concern in the
desperate soldier or the blear-eyed scholar (I: 39, 235–36, S177–78);
intellectual arrogance in the people "who perch astride the epicycle
of Mercury" (II: 17, 617, S481); dogmatism in the donkey, grave,
contemplative, disdainful, cocksure (III: 8, 917, S717); complacency
in the colleague who, after sweating his way through a stupid
speech, was heard in the lavatory conscientiously giving the credit
not to himself but to God (III: 10, 1000, S782); narcissism in the
friend who kept his diary only by his chamber pots, and in whose
nostrils all other conversation stank (III: 9, 922–23, S721).

Montaigne's love of metaphor extends constantly to his verbs.
His program for humiliating man and his reason in the "Apology,"
for example, is to *crush* and *trample underfoot* human arrogance
and pride; to *wrest* from men's hands the puny weapons of their
reason; to make them *bow their heads* and *bite the ground* beneath
the authority and reverence of the divine majesty.[7]

Whereas here Montaigne's metaphors emerge in related strings,
elsewhere they are often unrelated except insofar as one leads him
on to the next:

> *On ne cesse de criailler à nos oreilles, comme qui verseroit dans un*
> *antonnoir . . . Je voudrois qu'il corrigeast cette partie, et que, de*

*belle arrivée, selon la portée de l'ame qu'il a en main, il commençast
à la mettre sur la montre, luy faisant gouster les choses, les choisir et
discerner d'elle mesme; quelquefois luy ouvrant chemin, quelquefois
le luy laissant ouvrir. . . .*

*Il est bon qu'il le face trotter devant luy pour juger de son train,
et juger jusques à quel point il se doibt ravaler pour s'accommoder
à sa force. . . . Je marche plus seur et plus ferme à mont qu'à val.*
(I: 26, 149, S110.)

[They never stop bawling into our ears, as though they were pour-
ing water into a funnel . . . I should like the tutor to correct this
practice, and right from the start, according to the capacity of the
mind he has in hand, to begin putting it through its paces, making it
taste things, choose them, and discern them by itself; sometimes
clearing the way for him, sometimes letting him clear his own
way. . . .

It is good that he should have his pupil trot before him, to judge
the child's pace and how much he must stoop to match his strength.
. . . I walk more firmly and surely uphill than down.]

Most of the passages we have noted illustrate more than one
aspect of Montaigne's imagery. Here is one that combines several—
simile, a kind of metonymy, above all metaphor and personification
—in a vivid account of an older man's dialogue with his mind as
he strives to resist the encroachments of age:

*Puisque c'est le privilege de l'esprit de se r'avoir de la vieillesse, je
luy conseille, autant que je puis, de le faire; qu'il verdisse, qu'il
fleurisse ce pendant, s'il peut, comme le guy sur un arbre mort. Je
crains que c'est un traistre: il s'est si estroittement affreré au corps
qu'il m'abandonne à tous coups pour le suyvre en sa necessité. Je le
flatte à part, je le practique pour neant. J'ay beau essayer de le
destourner de cette colligeance, et luy presenter et Seneque et Catulle,
et les dames, et les dances royales; si son compagnon a la cholique, il
semble qu'il l'ait aussi. Les operations mesmes qui luy sont particu-
lieres et propres ne se peuvent lors souslever; elles sentent evidem-
ment au morfondu. Il n'y a poinct d'allegresse en ses productions, s'il
n'en y a quand et quand au corps.* (III: 5, 821, S641.)

[Since it is the privilege of the mind to rescue itself from old age, I
advise mine to do so as strongly as I can. Let it grow green, let it
flourish meanwhile, if it can, like mistletoe on a dead tree. I fear it is
a traitor. It has such a tight brotherly bond with the body that it
abandons me at every turn to follow the body in its need. I take it
aside and flatter it, I work on it, all for nothing. In vain I try to turn
it aside from this bond, I offer it Seneca and Catullus, and the ladies,
and the royal dances; if its companion has the colic, it seems to have

it too. Even the activities that are peculiarly its own cannot then be aroused; they evidently smack of a cold in the head. There is no sprightliness in its productions if there is none in the body at the same time.]

To quote Sainte-Beuve again, "The seam between the idea and the image is so deep inside that you neither see it nor think of it: thought and image, in him all are one . . ." [8] The most remarkable thing about Montaigne's teeming images—and indeed about his style—is that not one is merely an ornament; each one is part of the very shape and substance of his thought.

XI

DESTINY

In the nearly four centuries since his death, the image of Montaigne has evolved much as he did himself.[1] His contemporaries admired him mainly as a Stoical, sententious author of fine sayings. The seventeenth century saw him mainly as a Pyrrhonistic skeptic who preached and practiced the ideal of the *honnête homme.* Rousseau and many later Romantics were struck mostly by his self-portrait. In the nineteenth century Sainte-Beuve saw the importance of his natural, independent morality; and this feature has been stressed by a century of readers down to Gide and others in the present day.

Although the 1580 *Essais* were very well received, the 1588 version —as Marie de Gournay noted with indignation in 1595—aroused three criticisms in particular: for fabrication of new words; for rambling order; and for the whole enterprise of self-portrayal. Even Montaigne's perceptive friend Estienne Pasquier, who calls the *Essais* a masterpiece and his favorite reading, grants that these are faults and tells how he once tried vainly to persuade Montaigne to correct his Gasconisms. He regards Book III as the weakest, almost calling it a product of Montaigne's dotage; he praises the work mainly as *"un vray seminaire de belles et notables sentences"* ["a real seed-bed of fine and notable sayings"] and the author as "un autre Seneque en nostre langue" ["another Seneca in our language."] [2]

Many of Montaigne's early readers, however, were most impressed by his skeptical questioning of man's powers and place in the universe. It was partly this that led to the borrowings in England (soon noted by Ben Jonson) by Bacon, Marston, Webster, Burton, and even Shakespeare. Montaigne's fideism, or faith founded on skepticism about human knowledge, which the papal censors had passed over without comment in 1581, became for three-quarters of a century a popular though unofficial argument of the Counter Reformation against the Protestant trust in individual conscience and reason.[3] Here Montaigne was seconded by two disciples, Jean-Pierre Camus in his youthful *Essai sceptique* [*Skeptical Essay*] (1603), and Pierre Charron.

Charron (1541–1603), a fiery and successful preacher, was a friend of Montaigne and drew on him freely. His *Trois Veritez* [*Three Truths*] (1593) seeks to prove the existence of God, man's need of religion, and the truth of Catholicism against all other religions and sects, especially (with a heavy debt to Montaigne's skepticism) against Protestantism. In his main work, *De la sagesse* [*Of Wisdom*] (1601), he either paraphrases or quotes Montaigne, almost verbatim, without acknowledgment, at every turn. The first of its three books, on the knowledge of man, is taken almost entirely from Montaigne's demonstration of human vanity, weakness, inconstancy, misery, and presumption. What he borrows is typical of his time: Montaigne's early views, Stoical and skeptical, concerned with man's absurdity, not his dignity. He rejects the self-portrait, the play with ideas, the graceful irregularity, the serene acceptance of the human condition. Thus even in his most literal borrowings he changes Montaigne— perhaps without conscious intent—by making his ideas methodical, rigid, even dogmatic. Montaigne's distinction between religious belief and morality becomes a gulf in Charron.

This last distinction, born of the wars of religion, came in peacetime to seem a scandalous impiety. Four years after its publication, in 1605, *La Sagesse* was placed on the Index of Prohibited Books. However, it continued to be widely published and read, and did much to disseminate Montaigne's ideas.

The challenge of Montaigne's skepticism to seventeenth-century France is evident in two great readers, Descartes and Pascal.[4] Both start from it, Descartes in quest of certainty, Pascal of faith. In his *Discours de la méthode* [*Discourse on Method*] Descartes moves, as Montaigne often does, from disarming autobiography to firm assertion, from *"my* method" to *"the* method." He tells of abandoning fallible books to seek the truth within himself; adopts a provisional morality much like Montaigne's; and founds his basic concept, *"Je pense, donc je suis"* ["I think, therefore I am"], on the action of doubting, since this doubting is also an act of thought and thus incontrovertible proof of being. Even their many vast differences, such as Descartes's rejection of sense perception and of animal intelligence, show that for him Montaigne was the man to reckon with and refute.

Montaigne is even more important to Pascal as the ancestor and model of a type profoundly resistant to genuine piety, the *honnête homme.* In his interview with M. de Sacy, when he seeks admission to the austere Jansenist society of Port-Royal, Pascal appears as the man of two authors who knew man well but only partially and who do not complete but nullify each other: Epictetus, who saw man's greatness, and Montaigne, who saw man's misery. In his unfinished apology for Christianity, the *Pensées,* Pascal borrows heavily from Montaigne to prove our weakness, ignorance, and boredom, and thus to show that in religion, where reason can only point the way, we have nothing to lose by the wager of faith.

For all these borrowings and the fideism that they hold—however differently—in common, Montaigne remains what Sainte-Beuve aptly called the fox in Pascal's bosom; for even Pascal's eloquence cannot *prove* that his "misery of man," which is Montaigne's "human condition," must give rise to his distress and not to Montaigne's cheerful acceptance. He makes a magnificent case, especially in his analysis of boredom as the center of the human soul; but Montaigne had faced this problem and accepted it, and in another century Voltaire was to take his side in a debate that will surely never end.[5]

Montaigne left a varied legacy to the seventeenth century. As Pascal saw, he was the main educator and prototype of the *honnête homme.* For the common sixteenth-century ideal of the humanist, the learned bourgeois, he substituted that of the wellborn man of judgment, taste, and experience.[6] Perhaps most important, he focused man's attention on the human psyche. Both Descartes and Pascal based their cases for knowledge and faith on the workings of the soul; others in Montaigne's debt include La Fontaine, Mme.

de Sévigné, La Rochefoucauld, La Bruyère, and Molière. The great line of French *moralistes* springs from him. More than any other man, he set a great literature to studying the conduct and condition of man.

Then, late in the century, his impact weakened; his *Essais* were not republished between 1669 and 1724; and in 1676 (as we have noted), probably because of a growing mistrust of fideism, his popularity among freethinkers, and his bad press among theologians —Pascal, Nicole, Arnauld, Bossuet, and Malebranche—the *Essais* were placed on the Index. Perhaps an even greater cause of his disfavor was the growing concern with regularity and decorum.

In the eighteenth century Montaigne's lack of method and of regular order made him seem capricious and naïve. Many considered modernized versions the only way to correct his outdated language; only two regular editions appeared (though each was often reprinted), one of them in England. More a name than a figure to reckon with, Montaigne was often mentioned, less often read. His place on the Index and use by freethinkers led to a stereotype popularized by Voltaire, that of a naïve, almost primitive sage, a basically antireligious prototype of the *philosophes*, who in a time of cruel fanaticism had the wisdom and the courage to doubt.

However, he still had some readers of choice. Montesquieu praises him as a poet in prose and rejoices to see in him not man writing but man thinking. Diderot read him all his life and used him often.[7] While he regrets Montaigne's disbelief in man's capacity to know the universe, he shares one of his reasons for skepticism: the sense of the contrast between the flux of existence and the static formulas of language. Most of all he loves the vigor and vividness of Montaigne's organic, associative style; and in morality and esthetics he shows a similar openmindedness by his use of the dialogue form.

Rousseau uses Montaigne far more than he mentions him, but more early in his career than late. He draws on Montaigne's ironic critique of civilization in his own vehement attack and shares Montaigne's ideal of a pleasant, rounded education that involves judging and doing. For all their vast differences in aim and temperament—Montaigne's detached inquiry and concern with representativeness, Rousseau's proud confession and stress on his own uniqueness—Rousseau is acutely conscious of Montaigne and eager to outdo him as he writes his *Confessions,* which opened the floodgates of self-portrayal and incidentally legitimized that of Montaigne.

Despite Montaigne's pages on friendship, most nineteenth-century Romantics were repelled by his appeal to the judgment not the heart and pronounced him cold and insensible. At the same time, their quest for preneoclassical ancestors and their whole new esthetic renewed his popularity. His spontaneity and love of nature, his organic order and concreteness, came to seem riches, not defects, and his thought and style were no longer regarded as naïve and capricious but as rich and profound. As we noted before, his style now found admirers on every side—Chateaubriand, Nodier, Stendhal, George Sand, Mérimée, Michelet, Flaubert, and Sainte-Beuve in France (to name only some of the most outstanding), in England and America Byron, Hazlitt, Landor, Thackeray, Stevenson, Pater, and Emerson.

In many admirers the feeling for Montaigne went beyond the style to the man. Flaubert steeped himself in the *Essais,* found in them strength and serenity, wished he could have a chat with the person he called a foster father, and marveled at all the tastes, opinions, even manias, that they had in common. Emerson wrote of his first reading that the book spoke so sincerely to his thought and experience that it seemed to him he had written it himself in some former life.

Sainte-Beuve was both influenced and influential. We have noted his perceptive delight in Montaigne's style. He first met him head on in his early thirties when, still hankering for religion, he began his study of the Jansenism of Port-Royal and, coming to Pascal, found Montaigne in his path. Trying to see him through Pascal's eyes and seeing him instead through those of his own disillusionment, he pronounced him a tempting enchanter who undermined Christianity while pretending to defend it, disdained repentance, and embodied all man's forgetfulness of God: in short, "la Nature au complet, sans la Grâce" ["Nature complete without Grace"].

After the *Port-Royal* Sainte-Beuve resigned himself to sharing Montaigne's supposed incapacity for belief and never again charged him with perfidy. He considered him a perfect skeptic and disillusioned sage, hailed him as one of his masters, and relished his healthy zest for life:

Quel naturel heureux, curieux, ouvert à tout, détaché de soi et du chez-soi, déniaisé, guéri de toute sottise, purgé de toute prévention. Et quelle sérénité, quelle allégresse même, jusque dans la souffrance et dans les maux! que d'accortise à tout venant! que de bon sens partout! que de vigueur de pensée! quel sentiment de la grandeur, quand il y a lieu! que de hardiesse et aussi d'adresse en lui! J'appelle Montaigne "le Français le plus sage qui ait jamais existé." 8

[What a happy nature, curious, open to everything, detached from himself and the parochial, freed from illusion, cured of all stupidity, purged of all prejudice. And what serenity, indeed what blitheness, even in suffering and pains! What affability to all comers! What good sense in all matters! What vigor of mind! What a feeling for greatness, when appropriate! What boldness in him, and skill as well! I call Montaigne "the wisest Frenchman that ever lived."]

In the nineteenth century Montaigne became fully recognized, in all his aspects, as a great French writer. Meanwhile an extraordinary period of Montaigne scholarship began in the 1840's, lasted until World War I, and has scarcely flagged since. Villey and Strowski, with their demonstrations of an evolving Montaigne, showed that his thought was responsible and consistent. Research produced a truer sense of the time, the man, and the book. His fideism emerged as an anti-Protestant Catholicism not unusual in his time, his nonchalance about public affairs as mainly a corrective. Our picture of him today, despite many gaps, is clear and firm.

Montaigne's public today is worldwide. Excellent scholarly studies have come from Denmark, Holland, Italy, Germany, Japan, and the English-speaking countries; he may be read in Polish, in Russian, and in Turkish. His countless French admirers range from Alain to Anatole France, Maurois to Malraux, Butor to Montherlant. Albert Thibaudet saw him as an ancestor of his other literary hero, Bergson, edited him, and studied him with loving insight. American devotees, from Justice Holmes to Eric Hoffer, are equally diverse. Many aspects of Montaigne appeal to his readers. T. S. Eliot considered him a very great figure, founder of the distinguished French line of honest moralists, a universal skeptic who somehow succeeded in expressing the skepticism of every man.9 Aldous Huxley shows his greatness as the creator of the essay: "one damned thing after another" in a marvel of "free association artistically controlled." 10 Herbert Lüthy salutes him perceptively as a master of "the art of being truthful." Stefan Zweig, who started a book on Montaigne but did not live to finish it, saw him as the patron saint of every free man.

Besides his style, Montaigne's greatest attractions for readers today seem to be his honesty, his self-portrait that mirrors us all, and his mastery of the art of living. Virginia Woolf tells how century after century finds a crowd before his portrait, "gazing into its depths, seeing their own faces reflected in it, seeing more the more they look." For having achieved happiness through "a miraculous adjustment of all these wayward parts that constitute the human soul," she pronounces him a "great master of the art of life." [11] André Gide, one of Montaigne's greatest admirers, read him over and over with deep satisfaction and joy. Above all his other ideas he took this one for his own: *"l'estre veritable est le commencement d'une grande vertu"* ["to be truthful is the beginning of a great virtue"]. He rejoiced that Montaigne, as he put it, answered Pilate's atrocious question with his own purely human version of Jesus' answer, *"I* am the truth." For him the *Essais* were the book in which, like himself, every reader finds himself. *"A quel point je le fais mien . . . il me semble que c'est moi-même. . . . En lui chaque lecteur des* Essais *se reconnaît."* ["To what a point I make him my own . . . it seems to me that he is myself. . . . In him each reader of the Essays recognizes himself."] [12]

Montaigne is highly skeptical of many of our modern faiths: in medicine, science in general, and progress, in the perfectibility of our knowledge, in social and governmental change, in the equality of man, in our conviction that involvement is a virtue. Yet he seems to have many friends and alarmingly few enemies. While he had a low capacity for hostility and a disarming way of presenting his ideas, there seem to be other reasons for this.

He has a deep and abiding sense of our absurdity which, though it lacks anguish and does not deny man's dignity, still strikes a chord in the modern sensibility. Keenly aware of the wayward parts of our psyche, he has a psychiatrist's mistrust of hidden inner conflicts, and seeks wholesouledness, since without it we often act at our own risk and at that of others. Despite his religious faith, he is overwhelmingly concerned with the here and now. In man and in all creation he is less conscious of permanence than of change. Constantly striving for perspective, he is a devotee of cultural relativism. He rejects set rules of order and esthetics for the sake of something more organic. Convinced that each man must find his own answers to the questions and problems of life, he seeks to help men to do so.

Like most cultural relativists, he places a premium on honesty and truth. His self-portrait is not always candid, for it must show his own wit, modesty, and playful love of paradox; but he tries to make it wholly truthful. Communication is perhaps his deepest need; and he finds communication impossible without honesty. A generous heart, he writes, wants to reveal even its inmost depths; for there everything is good, or at least everything is human (II: 17, 630, S491). In short, for him the fundamental virtue is truth. *"La verité . . . est la premiere et fondamentale partie de la vertu. Il la faut aymer pour elle mesme. . . . Nous ne sommes hommes et ne nous tenons les uns aux autres que par la parole."* ["Truth is the first and fundamental part of virtue. We must love it for itself. . . . We are men, and hold together, only by our word."] (II: 17, 631, S491; I: 9, 37, S23.)

Perhaps what draws us more than anything to Montaigne today is not something we share—or even think we share—with him, but on the contrary something we lack, know we lack, and cannot stop yearning for: the scandalous serenity of his self-acceptance. In our age of guilt, full of men judging and feeling themselves judged, it is a source of hope and strength to hear a man who can say, and mean it:

> *J'ay mes loix et ma court pour juger de moy, et m'y adresse plus qu'ailleurs. . . . Si j'avois à revivre, je revivrois comme j'ay vescu; ny je ne pleins le passé, ny je ne crains l'advenir.* (III: 2, 785, 794, S613, 620.)
> [I have my own laws and court to judge me, and I address myself to them more than anywhere else. . . . If I had to live over again, I would live as I have lived. I have neither tears for the past nor fears for the future.]

৺§ APPENDIX I ৪৶

CHRONOLOGY

MAJOR EVENTS AND DATES IN MONTAIGNE'S LIFE

1533	February 28: Birth of Michel Eyquem de Montaigne.
1534–39	Montaigne, as infant, taught Latin and no French.
1539–46	Studies at the Collège de Guyenne in Bordeaux.
1557–70	Councillor in the Parlement of Bordeaux.
1559–63	Friendship with Etienne de La Boétie.
1565	Marriage to Françoise de La Chassaigne.
1568	Father Pierre dies. Michel now Lord of Montaigne.
1569	Translation of Sebond's *Theologia Naturalis*.
1570–71	Retirement, first work on *Essais*.
1572–76	Attempted mediation between Navarre and Guise.
1576	Medal struck bearing scales in balance.
1578	First attack of the kidney stone.
1580	First edition of *Essais* (Books I–II).
1580–81	Travels in Switzerland, Germany, and mainly Italy.
1581–85	Mayor of Bordeaux for two terms.
1586–87	Flight from the plague. Conferences at Saint-Brice. Visit from Navarre after Coutras.
1588	Trip to Paris as negotiator between Navarre and Henry III. First edition of all three books of *Essais*. Meets Marie de Gournay. Attends Estates-General of Blois.
1590	Invited to court by Henry IV; too ill to go.
1592	September 13: Death of Michel de Montaigne.

IMPORTANT EVENTS AND DATES OF MONTAIGNE'S TIME

1534	Rabelais: *Gargantua*. Affair of the Placards.
1536	Calvin: *Institutio Religionis Christianae*.

1540 Papal recognition of the Society of Jesus.

1545–52 Council of Trent (also 1562–63).

1547 Henry II succeeds Francis I as King of France. Birth of Cervantes.

1549–50 First books of Ronsard and Du Bellay.

1553 Death of Rabelais.

1555–56 Abdication of Charles V as King of Spain and Emperor. Philip II and Ferdinand I succeed.

1558–1603 Elizabeth Queen of England.

1560–74 Charles IX King of France. Power of Queen Mother, Catherine de' Medici.

1562–94 Religious civil wars in France.

1564 Death of Calvin. Birth of Galileo and Shakespeare.

1572 Massacre of Saint Bartholomew's Day.

1574–89 Henry III King of France.

1576 Formation of the Holy League.

1584 Henry of Navarre heir to throne of France. Power and intransigeance of the League.

1585–89 War of the Three Henries.

1588 Spanish Armada. Day of the Barricades in Paris. Killing of Henri de Guise by order of Henry III.

1589 Death of Catherine de' Medici. Assassination of Henry III; Henry of Navarre succeeds him as Henry IV.

1593–94 Abjuration, then coronation of Henry IV.

ఆ§ APPENDIX II §ఐ

FURTHER READING

EDITIONS

Essais. Ed. Dezeimeris and Barckhausen. Bordeaux: Gounouilhou, 1870–73, 2 vols. Reproduces 1580 version (Books I–II) and variants of 1582 and 1587.

Essais. Edition Municipale, by Fortunat Strowski *et al.* Bordeaux: Pech, 1906–33, 5 vols. Gives all variants of the six basic texts.

Essais. Edition Phototypique by Fortunat Strowski. Paris: Hachette, 1912, 1024 plates. Phototypic reproduction of Bordeaux Copy, showing all Montaigne's handwritten additions of 1588–92.

Œuvres complètes. Pléiade edition by Albert Thibaudet and Maurice Rat. Paris: Gallimard, 1962; 1965 printing preferred. Excellent and handy. Gives strata indicators.

Essais. Ed. by Pierre Villey, re-ed. by V.-L. Saulnier. Paris: Presses Universitaires de France, 1965. Excellent scholarly reader's edition. Gives strata indicators and dates of composition.

Complete Works. Trans. and ed. Donald M. Frame. Stanford, California: Stanford University Press, 1957. Also *Complete Essays.* Stanford, California: Stanford University Press, 1958 (hardcover), 1965 (paperback). Gives strata indicators.

STUDIES

Auerbach, Erich, "L'Humaine Condition," in *Mimesis,* trans. Willard R. Trask. Garden City: Doubleday & Company, Inc., 1957, pp. 249–73. Penetrating analysis of beginning of "Repentance" (III: 2).

Buffum, Imbrie, "The Basic Baroque Categories as Exemplified by Montaigne," in *Studies in the Baroque from Montaigne to*

Rotrou. New Haven: Yale University Press, 1957, pp. 1–76. Sensitive study of thought and style.

Emerson, Ralph Waldo, "Montaigne; or, the Skeptic," in *Representative Men.* Boston: Houghton Mifflin Company, 1903 ed., pp. 147–86. Sympathetic treatment of skepticism and assessment of Montaigne.

Frame, Donald M., *Montaigne: A Biography.* New York: Harcourt, Brace & World, Inc., 1965.

Friedrich, Hugo, *Montaigne.* Bern: Francke, 1949. In German. Full of superb insights into form as well as attitudes and ideas.

Gray, Floyd, *Le Style de Montaigne.* Paris: Nizet, 1958. Good study of many aspects.

Lanson, Gustave, *Les Essais de Montaigne: Etude et analyse.* Paris: Mellottée, 1930. Good all-round analysis, especially strong on Montaigne's skepticism.

Lüthy, Herbert, "Montaigne, or the Art of Being Truthful," *Encounter,* Nov., 1953, pp. 33–44; reprinted in Quentin Anderson and Joseph A. Mazzeo, *The Proper Study.* New York: St. Martin's Press, Inc., 1962, pp. 319–36. Brilliant treatment of Montaigne's self-portrait.

Sainte-Beuve, C.-A., *Port-Royal.* Paris: Hachette, 3rd ed., 1867–71, 7 vols. Vol. II (Livre III), 379–453. "Montaigne en voyage," in *Nouveaux Lundis.* Paris: M. and C. Lévy, 2nd–6th eds., 1870–83, 14 vols. Vol. II, 156–77. A specious but vivid portrait of a perfidious Montaigne, with fine pages on his style; and an enthusiastic account of his zest for travel and for life.

Thibaudet, Albert, *Montaigne.* Ed. Floyd Gray. Paris: Gallimard (NRF), 1963. Especially valuable for pre-Bergsonian "mobilism" in Montaigne.

Villey, Pierre, *Les Sources et l'évolution des Essais de Montaigne.* Paris: Hachette, 1908, 2 vols. 2nd revised ed., 1933, 2 vols. Masterly dating of Montaigne's writings and theory of development of his ideas, attitudes, and style.

Zeitlin, Jacob, Introduction and Notes to his translation of Montaigne, *Essays.* New York: Alfred A. Knopf, Inc., 1934–36, 3 vols. One of the most searching treatments of Montaigne.

◄§ NOTES §►

Chapter I   THE BOOK

[1] Montaigne, *Œuvres complètes* (Pléiade ed., Paris: Gallimard, 1962). The English edition of reference is my translation of the *Complete Works* and the *Complete Essays* (Stanford, Calif.: Stanford University Press, 1957, 1958; *Complete Essays* in paperback, 1965; same pagination in all three). References will appear in this form:

III: 2, 786, S614

meaning *Essais*, Book III, ch. 2, p. 786 (*Œuvres complètes*), p. 614 (*Complete Works* or *Complete Essays*).

References to the *Travel Journal* and the *Letters* are, of course, not found in my translation of the *Complete Essays*, but only in that of the *Complete Works*.

Wherever a passage is quoted which was published in 1580 and modified later, it appears here in its original form, not in that given by the editions of reference; and a further reference is given, usually in the following form, to the Dezeimeris and Barckhausen edition (DB):

II: 3, 334, S254; cf. DB I, 289.

Chapter II   THE AUTHOR AND HIS TIME

[1] Montaigne's Protestant sister, Jeanne de Lestonnac, became the mother of a recently canonized Catholic saint of the same name. Montaigne's role in keeping young Jeanne in the Catholic fold was clearly recognized in the canonization proceedings. See Chapter VIII.

[2] Fuller details of Montaigne's life are found throughout his writings, especially *Essais* I: 26 (childhood and education), I: 28 (friendship), III: 5 (marriage), III: 9 (domesticity and travel), III: 10 (mayoralty), and III: 12 (siege of Castillon and plague). See also my *Montaigne: A Biography* (New York: Harcourt, Brace & World, Inc., 1965).

[3] See Roger Trinquet's magisterial article, "Les Deux Sources de la morale et de la religion chez Montaigne," *Bulletin de la Société des Amis de Montaigne*, IV, 13 (Jan.–March, 1968), 24–33.

[4] Both study and tower are well preserved today.

[5] For these criticisms, see Chapter VIII.

Chapter III THE DECISION TO WRITE

¹ For the chronology of the *Essais*, I am following Pierre Villey in *Les Sources et l'évolution des Essais de Montaigne* (Paris: Hachette, 1908, 2 vols.; 2nd ed., 1933, 2 vols.).

² II: 12, 473, S364. For a fuller treatment of Montaigne's changes of view on death and pain, see Chapter VII, pp. 61–62.

³ In 1588 Montaigne cut down this list of amenities and made other slight changes in this passage. See Chapter VII, p. 63.

Chapter IV SKEPTICISM: TEMPER AND TOOL

¹ See Edwyn Bevan, *Stoics and Sceptics* (Oxford: Clarendon Press, 1913); Philip P. Hallie: *Scepticism, Man, and God* and *The Scar of Montaigne* (Middletown, Conn.: Wesleyan University Press, 1964 and 1966). The last-named book (pp. 24–27 and *passim*) is valuable for its stress on skepticism as a philosophy of living. For Montaigne's use of skeptical doctrine, see Craig B. Brush, *Montaigne and Bayle: Variations on the Theme of Skepticism* (The Hague: Nijhoff, 1966); for the relation of his skepticism to the religious conflict, Richard H. Popkin, *The History of Scepticism from Erasmus to Descartes* (Assen, The Netherlands: Van Gorcum, 1960).

² This phrase is a post-1588 addition, but it expresses more precisely what Montaigne had said in his original version (II: 12, 493, S380; cf. DB II, 100).

³ In a 1588 addition Montaigne goes even further (II: 12, 514, S397). Sebond had argued at length that the universe is made for man; Montaigne puts a similar argument into the mouth (or beak) of a gosling.

⁴ Louis Cons, *Anthologie littéraire de la Renaissance française* (New York: Holt, Rinehart & Winston, Inc., 1931), p. 143.

⁵ See my article "Did Montaigne Betray Sebond?" in *Romanic Review*, XXXVIII (1947), 297–329.

Chapter V THE SUBJECT AS SELF: THE ESSAY

¹ II: 6, 350–51, S267–68; cf. 352, 355, S271, and DB I, 303–5, 309. For similar uses of *essayer* in other chapters, see I: 20, 89, S63; I: 23, 116, S84–85, cf. DB I, 77; II: 12, 521, S403, cf. DB II, 116; II: 12, 543, S421.

² For a fuller discussion of the term and concept *essais* in Montaigne, see Chapter IX.

³ II: 17, 640, S498; cf. DB II, 235. After 1588 Montaigne changed the name of the ability he claimed from "judgment" to "sense."

⁴ I: 26, 147, S108; II: 8, 364, S278, cf. DB I, 317–18; II: 17, 636–37, S495–96, cf. DB II, 231–32; II: 37, 764, S596.

⁵ See Chapter VII, pp. 59–61.

Chapter VI THE SUBJECT AS MAN: BOOK III

¹ III: 5, 857–58, S670. After 1588 Montaigne changed *"naturelles"* ["natural"] to *"necesseres"* ["necessary"].

² See Frederick Kellermann's article "Montaigne's Socrates," *Romanic Review*, XLV (1954), 170–77, and his unpublished dissertation (Indiana University) on which the article is based.

³ III: 13, 1091, S852; cf. 1088, S851; 1096, S857.

⁴ III: 13, 1093–94, S854–55. After 1588 Montaigne made minor changes in the last sentence.

Chapter VII THE FINAL ADDITIONS

¹ I: 56, 303, 308–9, S229, 234; III: 10, 990, S775. The second of these additions was made before 1588.

² III: 2, 794, S619–20. Cf. below, p. 61.

³ For the first passage, see II: 12, 416, S320; cf. DB II, 18, and Edition Phototypique, plate 369. For the second, II: 12, 554, S429; cf. DB II, 152, and Edition Phototypique, plates 508–9.

⁴ I: 42, 252, S191. DB I: 217–18; also I: 18, 75, S52; I: 20, 82, S57–58; I: 21, 97, S70; I: 25, 134, S99; I: 27, 177–78, S132; I: 49, 284–85, S215; II: 27, 672, S524.

Some of these and the following references are not specifically to the *vulgar* but to the herd, the mob, or the rabble, by which Montaigne usually seems to mean the same thing.

⁵ II: 17, 618, S481; III: 2, 782, S611; III: 11, 1010, S790; III: 13, 1054, 1094, S824, 855. Most of these statements appeared in 1588.

Chapter VIII RELIGION

¹ *Journal de Voyage* [*Travel Journal*], Rome, March 20 and April 15, 1581; pp. 1228–29, 1240, S955–56, 965. Cf. my *Montaigne: A Biography*, pp. 217–18.

² The passages criticized are the following, or others like them: Fortune: II: 4, 346, S263. Heretic poets (Beza, Buchanan): II: 17, 645, S502. Julian the Apostate: II: 19, *passim*. Prayer: I: 56, *passim*. Cruelty: I: 31, 207–8, S155; II: 11, 410, S314. Doing good only from free choice: I: 26, 166, S123.

For the two added passages, see I: 56, 308, S234 (on fortune), and III: 10, 990, S775 (on heretic poets); for the disavowal, I: 56, 303, S229.

³ Pierre Villey, *Montaigne devant la postérité* (Paris: Boivin, 1935), chs. 5, 8, 10, 12, and *passim*; Alan M. Boase, *The Fortunes of Montaigne. A History of the Essays in France, 1580–1669* (London: Methuen & Co. Ltd., 1935), pp. 410–29 and *passim*; Richard H. Popkin, *The History of Scepticism from Erasmus to Descartes* (Assen, The Netherlands: Van Gorcum, 1960), chs. 3–6 and *passim*.

⁴ Maturin Dreano, *La Renommée de Montaigne en France au XVIIIe siècle, 1677–1802* (Angers: Editions de l'Ouest, 1952), pp. 552–53 and *passim*.

⁵ Sainte-Beuve, *Port-Royal*, II, 382–454 (Book III, chs. i–iii), especially pp. 406–9, 412–21, 425–31, 441–42. For a criticism of Sainte-Beuve's view, see my article "Did Montaigne Betray Sebond?" *Romanic Review*, XXXVIII (1947), 297–329. On Montaigne in the nineteenth century, see my *Montaigne in France, 1812–1852* (New York: Columbia University Press, 1940).

⁶ Two of the soundest treatments are Dreano's *La Pensée religieuse de Montaigne* (Paris: Beauchesne, 1936) and Armand Müller's *Montaigne* in the

series Les Ecrivains devant Dieu (Paris: Desclée de Brouwer, 1965). More extreme presentations, subject to caution, of a religious Montaigne, are Marc Citoleux's *Le Vrai Montaigne, théologien et soldat* (Paris: Lethielleux, 1937) and Clément Sclafert's *L'Ame religieuse de Montaigne* (Paris: Nouvelles Editions Latines, 1951).

⁷ See *Bulletin de la Société des Amis de Montaigne*, series 3, no. 9 (Jan.–March, 1959), pp. 4–5.

⁸ III: 13, 1079 and note, p. 1674, S844 and note; cf. Edition Phototypique, plate 1006. I: 56, 305, S232.

⁹ *Mémoire sur l'Edit de Janvier 1562* (Paris: Bossard, 1922).

¹⁰ Sebond, *Natural Theology*, ch. 208, conclusion. See my *Montaigne: A Biography*, pp. 110–11.

¹¹ See my *Montaigne: A Biography*, pp. 213–19. For a detailed debate on Montaigne's religious practice, see Maturin Dreano and Henri Busson in *Bibliothèque d'Humanisme et Renaissance*, XVI (1954), 86–95, 213–17.

¹² See Frieda S. Brown, *Religious and Political Conservatism in the Essais of Montaigne* (Geneva: Droz, 1963); and Marcel Raymond's article "L'Attitude religieuse de Montaigne" (originally entitled in part "Entre le fidéisme et le naturalisme") in his *Génies de France* (Neuchâtel: La Baconnière, 1942), pp. 50–67.

Chapter IX   THE ESSAIS: CONCEPT AND STRUCTURE

¹ For Montaigne's sense of the term *Essais*, see Andreas Blinkenberg, "Quel sens Montaigne a-t-il voulu donner au mot *Essais* dans le titre de son œuvre?" in *Bulletin de la Société des Amis de Montaigne*, III, 29 (Jan.–March, 1964), 22–32.

² Bacon used the title for his first *Essays*, published in 1597; but his other borrowings from Montaigne appear only in his later *Essays* and through the Florio translation of Montaigne, published in 1603.

³ In his edition of the *Essais* (Paris: Union Générale d'Editions, 1964–65), 3 vols. There is one excellent scholarly study of the subject, Richard A. Sayce's article "L'Ordre des 'Essais' de Montaigne," *Bibliothèque d'Humanisme et Renaissance*, XVIII (1956), 7–22.

⁴ Sometimes a chapter is related to one theme of a neighboring one: the presumptuous diviners of I: 31 lead us to the Christians in I: 32 who claim to know the secret plans of God.

⁵ See Chapter IV, pp. 29–31.

⁶ DB II: 37, p. 364. Later editions delete "and discordance": II: 37, 766, S598.

⁷ Villey, *Les Sources et l'évolution des Essais de Montaigne*, 2nd ed. (Paris: Hachette, 1933), I, 411.

⁸ Among the many treatments of Montaigne's order within his chapters are Grace Norton, *Studies in Montaigne* (New York: The Macmillan Company, 1904); Elly Wittkower, *Die Form der Essays von Montaigne* (Berlin: Levy,

1935); Jean Thomas, "Sur la composition d'un essai de Montaigne" (III: 9), *Humanisme et Renaissance*, V (1938), 297–306; René Jasinski, "Sur la composition chez Montaigne," in *Mélanges . . . Henri Chamard* (Paris: Nizet, 1951), pp. 257–67; R. A. Sayce, "Baroque Elements in Montaigne," *French Studies*, VIII (1954), 1–16; W. E. Traeger, *Aufbau und Gedankenführung in Montaignes Essays* (Heidelberg: Winter, 1961); M. Baraz, "Sur la structure d'un essai de Montaigne" (III: 6), *Cahiers de l'Association Internationale des Etudes Françaises*, XIV (March, 1962), 263–74.

[9] Especially Jean Thomas. For both references see the preceding note.

[10] There is even an unintentional illustration of Montaigne's nobiliary vanity when he says that "most of his ancestors" were born at his château (948, S741). In fact, his only ancestor born there—as it would seem he must have known—was his father.

[11] The term *coche* was still used very loosely in Montaigne's time; the title might almost be translated "Of Vehicles."

[12] In "Cripples" (III: 11) the connection, though hidden for most of the chapter (1002–11, S784–91), is perfectly clear. The subject is our eagerness to theorize about the causes of facts before verifying the facts themselves; the title comes from the theory, which Montaigne once accepted as a truth, that cripples are best at making love. The structure of "Physiognomy" (III: 12) is rather similar, moving from the noble simplicity of Socrates to that of Montaigne's peasant neighbors, thence to some of the lessons to be derived from this, thence back to Socrates, to his facial homeliness, to that of La Boétie, and to Montaigne's good fortune in having a disarmingly honest appearance.

Chapter X STYLE

[1] *Representative Men* (Boston: Houghton Mifflin Company, 1903 ed.), p. 168.

[2] Among those I have found most useful are the following, listed in alphabetical order: Erich Auerbach, "L'Humaine Condition," in *Mimesis*, trans. Willard Trask (Garden City, N.Y.: Doubleday & Company, Inc., 1957), pp. 249–73; M. Baraz, "Les Images dans les *Essais* de Montaigne," *Bibliothèque d'Humanisme et Renaissance*, XXVII (1965), 361–94; Imbrie Buffum, *Studies in the Baroque from Montaigne to Rotrou* (New Haven: Yale University Press, 1957), pp. 1–76; Morris W. Croll, "Attic Prose: Lipsius, Montaigne, Bacon," in *Schelling Anniversary Papers* (New York: Century House, Inc., 1923), pp. 117–50, and "The Baroque Style in Prose," in *Studies in English Philology . . . in Honor of Frederick Klaeber* (Minneapolis: University of Minnesota Press, 1929), pp. 427–56; Floyd Gray, *Le Style de Montaigne* (Paris: Nizet, 1958); Gustave Lanson, "L'Art de Montaigne: l'art de 'se dire,'" in *L'Art de la prose* (Paris: Librairie des Annales, 1911), pp. 39–54; Zoe Samaras, "The Comic Element of Montaigne's Style" (unpublished dissertation, Columbia University, 1967); Richard A. Sayce, *Style in French Prose* (Oxford: Clarendon Press, 1953), and "Baroque Elements in Montaigne," *French Studies*, VIII (1954), 1–16; Walter Schnabel, *Montaignes Stilkunst, eine Untersuchung vornehmlich auf Grund seiner Metaphern* (Breslau and Oppeln: Priebatsch, 1930); Jean Starobinski, "Montaigne en mouvement," *Nouvelle Revue Française*, VIII (Jan.–Feb., 1960), 16–22, 254–66; Albert Thibaudet, *Montaigne* (Paris: Gallimard, 1963), pp. 471–566.

³ I am using these terms in a general, current sense; for Montaigne made no paragraph divisions in his work, and in his final years divided many of his longer sentences into sentences so short as to be often mere phrases.

⁴ Such as this one about Dionysius the Elder and his verses: "*Et ce que ses charriots ne feirent non plus rien qui vaille en la course, et que la navire qui rapportoit ses gens faillit la Sicile et fut par la tempeste poussée et fracassée contre la coste de Tarente, il [le peuple] tint pour certain que c'estoit l'ire des Dieus irritez comme luy contre ce mauvais poëme.*" ["And the fact that his chariots did not make any kind of showing in the races either, and that the ship bringing his men back missed Sicily and was driven and shattered by the tempest against the coast of Tarentum, they [the people] felt certain that this was the wrath of the gods, irritated, like themselves, against this bad poem."] (II: 17, 619, S482.)

⁵ *Port-Royal*, II, 443 (Book III, ch. iii).

⁶ For other examples of combined simile and metaphor, see most of the quotations that follow in our text and III: 8, 905, S707; III: 13, 1043, S816. For metaphor and personification, see the famous portrait of virtue in a lovely plain in I: 26, 160–61, S119.

⁷ II: 12, 426, S327. For other examples of metaphor in verbs, see II: 17, 641, S499; III: 9, 970, S758; III: 10, 989, S773–74.

⁸ *Port-Royal*, II, 444.

Chapter XI DESTINY

¹ For fuller treatments of Montaigne's destiny see Alan M. Boase, *The Fortunes of Montaigne: A History of the Essays in France, 1580–1669* (London: Methuen & Co. Ltd., 1935); Pierre Villey, *Montaigne devant la postérité* (Paris: Boivin, 1935); Maturin Dreano, *La Renommée de Montaigne en France au XVIIIe siècle, 1677–1802* (Angers: Editions de l'Ouest, 1952); Donald M. Frame, *Montaigne in France, 1812–1852* (New York: Columbia University Press, 1940); Charles Dédéyan, *Montaigne chez ses amis anglo-saxons* (Paris: Boivin, 1946, 2 vols.).

² "Lettre à Monsieur de Pelgé" (*Lettres*, XVIII, 1; written c. 1602, published 1619), in *Choix de lettres*, ed. D. Thickett (Geneva: Droz, 1956), pp. 46–47 and *passim*, pp. 43–49.

³ Richard H. Popkin, *The History of Scepticism from Erasmus to Descartes* (Assen, The Netherlands: Van Gorcum, 1960), pp. 66–67.

⁴ See Léon Brunschvicg, *Descartes et Pascal, lecteurs de Montaigne* (New York and Paris: Brentano, 1944).

⁵ Voltaire, *Remarques sur les Pensées de M. de Pascal* (1734).

⁶ See Boase, *The Fortunes of Montaigne*, pp. 307–58 and *passim;* Thibaudet, *Montaigne*, p. 49; René Pintard, *Le Libertinage érudit dans la première moitié du XVIIe siècle* (Paris: Boivin, 1943, 2 vols.), *passim;* Joachim Merlant, *De Montaigne à Vauvenargues* (Paris: Société Française d'Imprimerie et de Librairie, 1914), pp. 1–87 and *passim;* and especially Fortunat Strowski, *La Sagesse française* (Paris: Plon, 1925), pp. 31–32, 44–45, 50–51, 96, 105, and *passim;* and M. Magendie, *La Politesse mondaine et les théories de l'honnêteté, au XVIIe siècle, de 1600 à 1660* (Paris: Alcan, 1926, 2 vols.), I, 387–93; II: 791; and *passim*.

[7] See Jerome Schwartz, *Diderot and Montaigne. The Essais and the Shaping of Diderot's Humanism* (Geneva: Droz, 1966).

[8] "Montaigne en voyage" (March 24, 1862), in *Nouveaux Lundis* (Paris: M. and C. Lévy, 1870–83), II, 177.

[9] Introduction to Pascal, *Pensées* (Everyman Edition), pp. xiv–xv; also in *Essays Ancient and Modern*.

[10] Preface to *Collected Essays* (New York: Harper & Row, Publishers, 1958), p. vii.

[11] *The Common Reader* (New York: Harcourt, Brace & World, Inc., 1948 ed.), pp. 87, 100.

[12] "Essai sur Montaigne" and "Suivant Montaigne" in *Œuvres complètes* (Paris: Nouvelle Revue Française, 1933–39, 15 vols.), XV, 4–5, 45; *Les Pages immortelles de Montaigne* (Paris: Corrêa, 1948), pp. 10, 14–15. Some of these statements are found in English in *The Living Thoughts of Montaigne, Presented by André Gide* (New York and Toronto: Longmans, Green, 1939), pp. 1–27.

INDEX

A

Addison, 73
ÆEneid (Virgil), 16
Affaire des Placards, 5, 105
Alain, 102
Alexander (the Great), 49
Amboise, 5
America, 86, 101
Apollo, 32
Aristotle, 23, 44–45, 50
Armada, Spanish, 106
Armaingaud, Arthur, 66
Arnauld, Antoine, 100
Atticism, 86
Auerbach, Erich, 86, 90, 107, 113
Aulus Gellius, 17
Austria, 13

B

Bacon, Francis, 73, 97, 112
Baraz, M., 93, 113
Barckhausen, Henri, 2, 26, 28, 107
Barricades, Day of the, 106
Bastille, 15
Beauregard, Thomas de (Montaigne's brother), 67
Bergson, Henri, 102
Bevan, Edwyn, 110
Beza, 111
Blinkenberg, Andreas, 112
Boase, Alan M., 111, 114
Bordeaux, 1, 3, 6–8, 12–15, 42, 105
Bordeaux Copy (of Montaigne's *Essais*), 2, 53, 87, 107

Bordeaux Parlement: *see* Parlement of Bordeaux
Bossuet, 66, 100
Brach, Pierre de, 2
Brazil, 38
Brown, Frieda S., 112
Brunschvicg, Léon, 114
Brush, Craig B., 110
Brutus, 49
Buchanan, George, 111
Buffum, Imbrie, 86, 107, 113
Bunel, Pierre, 67
Burton, Robert, 97
Busson, Henri, 112
Butor, Michel, 74–75, 102
Byron, 101

C

Caesar, Julius, 49, 76
Calvin, 5, 105–6
Camus, Jean-Pierre, 98
Castillon, 6, 14, 42, 109
Cateau-Cambrésis, Treaty of, 5
Catherine de' Medici, 5, 12, 14–15; 106
Catholic(s), 4, 8, 17, 56, 67, 71
Catholicism, 25, 27, 67, 98, 102
Cato the Elder (the Censor), 49, 59
Cato the Younger (of Utica), 20, 22, 39; 49
Catullus, 95
Cellini, 4
Cervantes, 106
Chambre des Enquêtes, 9
Chambre des Requêtes, 9
Charles V, Emperor, 4, 5, 106

Charles IX, king of France, 5, 11–12, 106
Charron, Pierre, 98
Chartres, 15
Chateaubriand, 86, 101
Christian(s), 24, 68–69
Christianity, 27, 31, 48, 56, 66, 71, 78, 99, 101
Church, 13, 56, 65–66, 69, 71
Church Fathers, 71
Cicero, 19, 44–45, 77, 79
Citoleux, Marc, 112
Cognac, 14
Collège de France, 4
Collège de Guyenne, 9, 105
Collège des Lecteurs Royaux, 4, 9
Colloquy of Poissy, 5
Confessions (Rousseau), 101
Cons, Louis, 27, 110
Council of Trent, 68, 106
Counter Reformation, 98
Counter-Reformers, 66
Cour des Aides of Périgueux, 9
Coutras, 14, 105
Cowley, 73
Crinito, Pietro, 17
Croll, Morris W., 113

D

Dédéyan, Charles, 114
Delphi, 32
Denmark, 102
De Quincey, 73
Descartes, 66, 98; quoted, 99
Dezeimeris, Reinhold, 2, 26, 28, 107
Diderot, 86, 100
Dionysius the Elder, tyrant of Syracuse, 114
Discourse on Method (Descartes), 98
Discourses (Machiavelli), 3
Dordogne river, 7–8, 14
Dreano, Maturin, 111–12, 114
Du Bellay, Joachim, 106
Duns Scotus, 68
Duras, Madame Marguerite de, 80
Du Verdier, Antoine, 42

E

Ecclesiastes, 71

Edict of Nantes, 6
Egypt, 84
Eliot, T. S., 25, 102
Elizabeth I, queen of England, 106
Emerson, 25, 73, 101, 108; quoted, 86
England, 86, 97, 100–1
Epaminondas, 49, 51
Epictetus, 99
Epicurus, 23
Essai sceptique (J.-P. Camus), 98
Essais (Montaigne), passim
Estates-General of Blois (1588), 15, 105
Estissac, Louise d', 79
Europe, 4
Europeans, 44, 84
Eyquem (family), 3, 7, 8. (For individual members, see Montaigne)

F

Ferdinand I, Emperor, 5, 106
Ferdinand V, king of Spain, 7
Fielding, 73
Flaubert, 86, 101
France, 3–5, 9, 13, 42, 83, 86, 88, 98, 101, 106
France, Anatole, 102
Francis I, king of France, 4–5, 106
Francis II, king of France, 5
French, Frenchman, Frenchmen, 38, 82, 102
French (language), 8, 26, 105
Friedrich, Hugo, 108

G

Galileo, 106
Garasse, François, 66
Gargantua (Rabelais), 105
Gasconisms, 97
Gascony, 27, 88
Gaujac, Pierre de (uncle of Montaigne), 9
Geneva, 5
Germans, 68
Germany, 13, 102, 105
Ghibelline(s), 6
Gide, 66, 97; quoted, 103
God, 11, 24, 27–29, 31, 39, 48, 52, 58, 65–66, 69–71, 78, 84, 94, 98, 101
Goldsmith, 73

Gospels, 71
Gournay, Marie de, 2, 15, 97, 105
Gray, Floyd, 86, 108, 113
Greece, 19, 84
Greek (language), 9, 81
Greeks, 32, 84
Gregory XIII, Pope, 67
Guelph(s), 6
Guevara, Antonio de, 17
Guienne, 7
Guise, Henri de, 4, 6, 12, 15, 90–91, 105–6
Guise (family), 5, 6
Gurson, Diane de Foix, countess of, 80

H

Hallie, Philip P., 110
Hazlitt, William, 101
Henri de Guise: see Guise
Henry II, king of France, 5, 106
Henry III, king of France, 2, 4, 6, 12–15, 27, 42, 56, 90–91, 105–6
Henry IV, king of France (Henry of Navarre), 3–4, 6, 12, 14–15, 27, 56, 90–91, 105–6
Hoffer, Eric, 102
Holland, 102
Holmes, Oliver Wendell, Jr. (Justice), 102
Holy League: see League
Holy Roman Empire, 4–5
Horace, 63, 77
Huguenot, 90–91
Huxley, Aldous, quoted, 102

I

Imperials, 5
Index of Prohibited Books, 11, 13, 27, 66–67, 98, 100
Inquisition, 7
Institutes (Calvin), 5, 105
Isabella, queen of Spain, 7
Italian (language), 13
Italy, 4–5, 13, 102, 105

J

Jansenism, 101
Jansenists, 66

Japan, 102
Jasinski, René, 113
Jesuit, 68–69
Jesus, 103
Jews, 7
Johnson, Samuel, 73
Jonson, Ben, 97
Journal de Voyage (Montaigne): see Travel Journal Julian the Apostate, Emperor, 65, 75, 111

K

Kellermann, Frederick, 111

L

La Boétie, Etienne de, 3, 9–11, 16, 19, 22, 63, 67, 74, 105, 113
La Bruyère, 99
La Chassaigne, Françoise de: see Montaigne
La Croix du Maine, 3, 42
La Fère, 13
La Fontaine, 99
Lancre, Pierre de, 68
Landor, Walter Savage, 101
L'Angelier, Abel, 1–2
Lanson, Gustave, 108, 113
La Rochefoucauld, 99
Latin, 2, 8, 10–11, 81, 105
Latinists, 9
League, 4, 6, 14–15, 106
Leaguers, 14–15
Leonardo da Vinci, 4
Lestonnac, Jeanne de (Montaigne's sister), 67, 109
Lestonnac, Saint Jeanne de (Montaigne's niece), 66–67, 109
Liber Creaturarum, sive Theologia Naturalis (Sebond), see Natural Theology
Lidoire river, 8
Lipsius, Justus, 3, 42
Lopez de Villanueva, Micer Pablo, 7
Louppes, Antoine de, 8
Louppes, Antoinette de: see Montaigne
Louppes, Pierre de, 8
Loyola, Saint Ignatius of, 69
Lucca, 13
Lucretius, 19, 77
Lutheranism, 67

Lüthy, Herbert, 108; quoted, 102-3
Lysis (Plato), 78

M

Macaulay, 73
Machiavelli, 3
Magendie, M., 114
Maldonado, Juan, 68
Malebranche, 66, 100
Malraux, André, 102
Margaret of Valois: *see* Valois
Marot, 4
Marston, John, 97
Mass, 5, 15, 68
Master of the Sacred Palace (Sisto Fabri), 13, 27, 42, 65, 67
Matignon, Jacques de, marshal, 14-15, 42
Maurois, André, 102
Medici: *see* Catherine de' Medici
Mercury, 94
Mérimée, 86, 101
Merlant, Joachim, 114
Mersenne, Marin, 66
Mexia, Pedro de, 17
Michelet, 86, 101
Millanges, Simon, 1
Molière, 99
Montaigne (château and estate), 7-8, 11-12, 14, 105, 113
Montaigne, Antoinette de (mother), 7-8, 11
Montaigne, Françoise de (wife), 10, 105
Montaigne, Léonor de (daughter), 10
Montaigne, Michel de, *passim*
Montaigne, Pierre Eyquem de (father), 3, 7-8, 10-11, 19, 26, 67, 105
Montaigne, Ramon Eyquem de (great-grandfather), 7
Montesquieu, 86, 100
Montherlant, Henry de, 102
Moralia, or *Moral Essays* (Plutarch), 3
Müller, Armand, 111
Muses, 11

N

Natural Theology (Sebond), 3, 11, 26, 67, 105, 112
Naudé, Gabriel, 66

Navarre, Henry of: *see* Henry IV
New World, 44, 84
Nicole, Pierre, 100
Nodier, Charles, 101
Normandy, 13
Norton, Grace, 82, 112

O

Occam, 68
Ovid, 16

P

Pallas, 46
Papacy, 5
Paris, 1-2, 4-6, 9, 11-12, 15, 42, 83, 105
Parlement, the, 9
Parlement of Bordeaux, 3, 9-12, 67, 105
Parlement of Paris, 67
Pascal, 66, 69, 86, 98-101, 115
Pasquier, Estienne, 68, 97
Pater, Walter, 101
Patin, Guy, 66
Pavia, 4
Pensées (Pascal), 99, 115
Périgord, 7
Perigordians, 68
Périgueux, 9
Peru, 84
Phaedo (Plato), 51
Philip II, king of Spain, 5, 106
Pilate, 103
Pintard, René, 114
Pius XII, Pope, 66
Plato, 71, 78; *see* also *Phaedo*
Plattard, Jean, 2
Plautus, 16
Pléiade, 87
Pliny the Elder, 19, 32, 36, 55
Plutarch, 3, 10, 19, 71, 84
Popkin, Richard H., 110-11, 114
Port-Royal, 99, 101
Port-Royal (Sainte-Beuve), 24, 66, 101, 108, 111, 114
Posidonius, 23
Protestant(s), 5-6, 8, 13-15, 56, 67-68
Protestantism, 5-6, 10, 71, 98
Pyrrho, 30, 51
Pyrrhonism, 25, 27, 29-31
Pyrrhonists, Pyrrhonians, 29-30, 66

R

Rabelais, 4, 105–6
Rat, Maurice, 2, 107
Raymond, Marcel, 112
Renaissance, 4
Representative Men (Emerson), 25, 113
Rhodiginus, Coelius, 17
Richer, Jean, 1
Roman(s), 10, 84
Romantics, 86, 97, 101
Rome, 13, 19, 83–84
Ronsard, 106
Rouen, 15
Rousseau, 97, 100–1

S

Sacy, Monsieur de, 9
Sagesse, de la (Charron), 98
Saint Bartholomew's Day Massacre, 3;
    5–6, 19, 106
Saint-Brice, 14, 105
Sainte-Beuve, 24, 27, 66, 86, 97, 99,
    101, 108, 111; quoted, 93, 96, 102
Saint Michael, Collar and Order of
    (ordre du Roy), 1–2, 12
Samaras, Zoe, 87, 113
Sand, George, 86, 101
Saulnier, V.-L., 107
Sayce, Richard A., 112–13
Schnabel, Walter, 113
Schwartz, Jerome, 115
Scipio the Younger, 49
Sclafert, Clément, 112
Scripture, 70
Sebond, Raymond, 3, 11, 16, 26–28,
    31–33, 67, 69, 105, 110, 112
Seneca, 19, 23, 29, 36, 71, 77, 95, 97
Sévigné, Madame de, 99
Shakespeare, 98, 106
Sicily, 114
Society of Jesus, 106
Socrates, 30, 32, 39, 44, 49–51, 58–59;
    63, 78, 113
Sorbonne, 4
Spain, 5, 7, 106
Spaniard(s), 11, 28, 84
Spiritual Exercises (Loyola), 69
Staël, Madame de, 86
Starobinski, Jean, 86, 113
Steele, 73
Stendhal, 86, 101

Stevenson, Robert Louis, 73, 101
Stoic(s), 23–24, 50, 64
Stoicism, 59
Strowski, Fortunat, 2, 102, 107, 114
Switzerland, 13, 105

T

Tarentum, 114
Terence, 16
Thackeray, 101
Thales, 3, 42
Theologia Naturalis (Sebond): *see Natural
    Theology*
Thibaudet, Albert, 2, 86, 93, 102;
    107–8, 113–14
Thomas, Jean, 113
Thou, Jacques-Auguste de, 12
Toulouse, 8
Traeger, W. E., 113
Travel Journal (Montaigne), 13, 67;
    109, 111
Trinquet, Roger, 109
Trois Veritez (Charron), 98

U

University of Toulouse, 9

V

Valois, Margaret of, queen of Navarre;
    14, 26–28
Venice, 13
Venus, 51
Villa, baths of La, 13
Villey, Pierre, 2, 74, 102; 107–8;
    110–12, 114
Virgil, 16; quoted, 53
Voltaire, 99–100, 114
Voluntary Servitude (La Boétie); 74
Vulcan, 51

W

War of the Three Henries; 6; 106
Webster, John, 97
Webster's Dictionary, 73
Wittkower, Elly, 112
Woolf, Virginia, quoted, 103
World War I, 102

Z

Zeitlin, Jacob, 108
Zweig, Stefan, 103